All the Feelings
All at Once

A moderately inappropriate
parenting memoir in Facebook posts
by a mom who couldn't make this

up if she tried.

Trisha Hall-Mullèr

All the Feelings All at Once © 2019 by Trisha Hall-Muller. All rights reserved. No part of this book may be reproduced in any way without written permission from the publishers except by a reviewer who may quote brief passages to be printed in a website, newspaper, or magazine.

ISBN: 9781799015413

Cover design by Jonathan Feld.

Photos courtesy of the author.

https://scanticbooks.blogspot.com
Facebook: Scantic Books

Dedication

This book is lovingly dedicated to my dear friend, Kerri Thoelen, who lost a courageous and brave battle with breast cancer in 2014.

She made me promise that I would follow my dream to write a book and cross it off the first entry on my bucket list. She wanted the first signed copy.

I will keep my promise to you, my beautiful friend. Hot off the press, I will find a way to thank you for believing in me and pushing myself to make my dream become reality.

Until we learn to line dance together like we discussed so often and in excited anticipation … this is my gift to you.

Foreword

When I told a friend that Trisha Hall-Muller was writing a parenting memoir, she responded, "Great! I hope her book is as good as her Facebook posts. Those are terrific!" My friend is in luck. This book is composed almost entirely of Trisha's Facebook posts. In fact, we're all in luck to have this book.

I first met Trisha when she was a student in several of my classes at Asnuntuck Community College two decades ago. She struck me as bright, funny, open minded, and kind hearted. Now—after many years, several jobs, marriage and divorce, lots of education, and two wonderful children—she still has all of those qualities. But beyond that, she has developed a stunning writer's voice to express the inner life that most people can't put on paper—or, in Trisha's case, send into cyberspace.

Considering the immediacy of social media, it's remarkable that Trisha's Facebook posts hold up so in the more contemplative pace of a book. Her words were often dashed off at the end of hectic days to make sense of her experiences and share those experiences with online friends. These posts have been slightly edited and rearranged here for overall clarity, but they retain the immediacy, energy, and freshness that they had the moment Trisha clicked the "share" command.

In this book, Trisha explores a range of subjects. Her children, of course, are center stage. One is the soccer diva daughter, and the other is the Autism-spectrum son—but neither is limited by Trisha's writing to any stereotypical roles. Like her, both are intelligent, expressive, complex, and endearing. They are most often the primary focus of each event Trisha relates, but they're also hovering on the fringes when she writes about other aspects of her life. If she's mourning the loss of a close friend, recalling her own childhood, reflecting on her career as an educator, or digging into her own psychological makeup, her kids are always there, grounding her.

Trisha's strength as a writer is her ability to capture brief moments that might elude less observant eyes. She discovers the

—

4

essential human qualities of humor, insight, annoyance, or even pure love with precise description and distinct dialogue. She is a master of the vignette, able to find deeper meaning in fleeting moments: a commute to work, a dinner-table conversation, a walk on the beach, or a sidelong glance. Nothing escapes her notice, and she translates her observations into deeply affecting passages that might range from a single sentence to a full-length essay.

She does it all in a tone that pokes fun at herself and the world around her with biting commentary that always manages to avoid cruelty and pettiness while returning to hope and gratitude. Above all (and despite a range of common and uncommon life obstacles), this book is relentlessly optimistic in the most realistic way possible. Trisha's writing is a testament to the power of a good attitude—generously spiced with a keen eye for irony.

I'm always thrilled when Trisha posts on Facebook. I never know in advance what she has in store for her Facebook friends, but I always know it will be something as affecting as anything I might find in the library or bookstore. My favorite line in this book is when Trisha reveals the freedom she finds in writing: "I love to write because nobody tells me I talk too much." Not once in reading this book did I want her to stop expressing herself.

I'm happy and honored to invite everyone to delve into Trisha's world through this book. You could start at the beginning and use the traditional linear approach. Or feel free to dip a toe into whatever part of Trisha's literary pond looks most intriguing. Even flipping through the pages to various random destinations would be as rewarding as a casual scroll through the best Facebook timeline you ever encountered.

Whatever the method, no one with any sense will read this book and tell Trisha she talks too much.

John Sheirer
Professor of English and Communication
Asnuntuck Community College

This Story

This story is still half in my cranium and half in Facebook posts. It's a memoir of being a mom on the verge of needing a padded room while raising a soccer diva daughter and a big-hearted son on the Autism spectrum. It's all the feelings all at once.

Two Lines

In December of 2002, two lines appeared on a pregnancy test, and I learned that my life was about to change. I had no idea what I was doing, yet I knew I was about to be blessed and made whole.

In August of 2003 (five weeks early) after three days of terrifying labor, a tiny, bald baby boy was placed into my arms. I had no idea what I was doing, yet I knew I had been blessed and learned about love at first sight.

In 2007, I received the diagnosis for my beautiful, little boy. Our premonitions were more than gut instincts. The words rang out from the professionals like surreal knives to my soul.

My child had autism.

I had no idea what I was going to do, yet I knew I was blessed to be strong enough to fight for everything he would need to succeed.

Fast-forward to 2018. I have a fourteen-year-old son with Autism. I have a fourteen-year-old son with high honors and the most compassionate views about the world around him. I have a son who loves to make others smile, who strives to work harder than anyone to achieve academic perfection, a child who knows that he learns about the world differently, yet embraces the young man he has become. Who knows he is *different*, not *less*.

I still have no idea what I'm doing, yet I am blessed because he has taught me about being the kind of parent I don't think I would've been if he wasn't the miracle he is.

I have a son with Autism and I thank God every day that he was given to me to learn about the true meaning of life.

Twenty-One Weeks

Tomorrow is a special day for me.

Nine years and a few endless months ago, I was in my way to Central Connecticut State University for a grad school class when the symptoms began. The same symptoms that I had encountered right before I was induced almost a month early with my son. Symptoms that represent preeclampsia.

I was twenty-one weeks along.

To keep it short, I was hospitalized on bed rest with all the nasty fixings: meds to speed up my unborn child's lungs, meds to bring my ungodly blood pressure down, meds to treat my kidneys that were beginning to fail. Doctors pulled no punches explaining that, if she did survive a micro-preemie birth, we were in for the toughest road ahead we had ever known.

So I learned to pray. I prayed hard and often, keeping up with the rhythm of my racing heart, mind, and tears.

My body was so sick, and in return, my precious, tiny baby girl had to fight along with me. I had never felt so frightened and let down. If I couldn't keep her safe, what kind of mother was I?

Dylanie Sue Muller was born on August 3, 2005. She came into the world a month early as loud and strong as she is to this day. I like to think that she gets her strong will from her mom—who opted to do *whatever* it took to keep her safe.

As sick as I was, I would do it again ten times harder if it meant having that beautiful, funny, fresh little girl in my world.

With pride in my heart, even a day early, I want to tell my entire Facebook family that my little survivor, my mini-me, will be nine years old tomorrow. She is everything a little girl should be. The kind of girl who catches toads and torments ants in the backyard, yet paints her nails with glitter and dances around our house in sparkly dresses while forcing the family cat to wear doll clothes.

I treasure you, Lanie Sue. You make me crazy and full of the kind of love I could only have learned from your teachings.

Happy birthday to my miracle.

—

212 Over 167

Unlike a lot of moms, I loathed being pregnant. I didn't glow. I perspired—a lot. I waddled, peed when I blinked, grunted like a wild boar just trying to get out of my vehicle. I didn't have the voluptuous breasts most pregnant woman have. I looked like a combination of a National Geographic barbarian woman and a river map of fleshy veins and extra bulging "stuff." I envied those Earth-mother types that taught Swahili to their unborn future geniuses in utero. I just looked forward to peeing in the proper receptacles and pouring my girth into a pair of men's boxers at the end of the day.

I wanted a baby a few years into my marriage and wanted to coincide with my friend who had just gotten pregnant. I tracked my fertility online and immediately got pregnant with Logan. Call me Fertile Myrtle with my rockin' on the mommy cycle. Bam! Two lines—on the thirty something tests I peed upon because I wanted to be "absolutely sure."

My first pregnancy was a nightmare. I was diabetic early on and my sugars were sky rocking. At thirty-five weeks, my blood pressure went through the roof, and I was induced. After a three-day labor (wasn't allowed to talk, have lights on, or get out of bed—hello bed pan, goodbye any dignity) the fifteen meds in my IV finally kicked in. With a blood pressure reading of 212 over 167, I gave birth to a tiny, bald miracle named Logan Timothy. Bloated and resembling Fred Flintstone, I held this new miracle and finally knew I had the power within me to kill someone if anyone ever tried to cause him harm.

I got baby fever when Logan was sixteen months old and immediately got pregnant again. We found out at nineteen weeks we were having a baby girl. Typically, Dylanie was spread-eagle in the ultrasound, announcing her presence. At twenty-one weeks, I was admitted to the hospital with severe preeclampsia and stayed there on bed-rest, praying that she would survive. I never told anyone how scared I was. We lived week to week, growing a little girl whose fate was terrifyingly unknown. At thirty-five weeks, we were induced and, at a little after thirteen hours of labor, vomiting and cursing, a healthy, yet tiny, premature Dylanie Sue came into the world, screeching and taking her first tornado poop all over the delivery nurse. Some things don't change.

Random Gratitude List #1

In no particular order, here is an excerpt from my gratitude list, otherwise known as a "Trisha Muller cluster of random, yet heartfelt outbursts put into the printed word."

I am thankful for …

1. My children (because they're freaking awesome, obviously).

2. My family, immediate and extended. They love me for the glorious mess I am proud to be and love me still when I am less than lovable.

3. My friends, for they are sick and twisted like myself and accept (sometimes influence) my inability to be appropriate and filtered. My closest friends are those who know how to speak in codes and nicknames when we delight in keeping our most offensive stories out of earshot and nosy bystanders. (Examples include "the workout thumb, the noisy ass broken heater, monkey rule #6, dead on *Sling Blade* similarities, incoming drones" and more.)

4. Funny cat videos.

5. Funny flatulence videos.

6. Funny videos of people falling down.

7. The "F" word.

8. Videos of cats causing people to fall down, fart, and drop the "F" bomb.

9. Black leggings, slippers, sports bras, tie-dyed hoodies, sloppy hair buns, fuzzy socks, pizza, fire pit and Netflix weekends.

10. The fact that those who read this list will either be annoyed by my vocabulary choices and long-winded descriptions, put off because they just apparently hate life and have the sense of humor found in a fossilized mule turd, scratch their heads wondering what their special nickname is or if they have a claim to secret fame that can only be deciphered by few.

Or … They will appreciate the mere knowledge that they are loved and understood by this girl, and I am extremely grateful to

---

have found such rare, obscene, eccentric. and beautiful people in this world who I am proud to call my friends.

Happy Thanksgiving Day to all!

Go with the Flow

The theory that laughter is healing is so factual in my world. I sometimes forget to find gratitude in the fact that I don't need to go far to find humor. My children's world views and verbal, random life goals sometimes have me shaking my head with fear and pride that I've raised such funny little people.

During our morning commute to daycare, my daughter asked me if I wanted more children. When I explained that my family was complete, she responded with, "yeah, I figured you were going to say that. That's why I was scared to ask you for your credit card number when I found babies for sale online."

Not lying. Verbatim.

After nearly driving off the road and mentally telling myself that her "online shopping" apparently needs to be more a tad more closely monitored, she switched up the subject and told me how she wants to own a farm someday soon.

Benign enough, right?

Nope.

"I want to raise chickens on my farm. I can't wait to own a rooster so I can force it to mate with a hen and get baby chicks."

Wait. It gets better.

I made the mistake of asking her how she knows about mating. Notice I said mistake.

"Mom, you know I read about these things. You make the rooster mate with the hen, he fertilizes the egg, she lays the egg, sits on the egg, and there you go ... babies. They just go with the flow."

If anyone owns poultry and prefers them not to be made into farming sex slaves ... keep them away from my daughter.

The Point Is

I was diagnosed with Attention Deficit Hyperactivity Disorder (ADHD) at age twenty-nine. My entire life has been a struggle with knowing what I'm thinking and want to convey. My brain just happens to be wired in such a way that makes thinking a continental travel to every place except where I want to visit when trying to have a conversation.

It makes me come across to others as someone who talks too much, is way too hyper, and takes the road *wayyyyy* less traveled.

It's just hard sometimes battling with a brain that goes in every direction except the path it's supposed to be on.

I've come to a point where it's easier to love who I am than to try to fit into the mold of someone I can't be.

Writing is the only place I feel like I can purge my thoughts into more simplistic prose and terminology. I love to write because nobody tells me I talk too much.

I speak like I think. For those who find my conversations frustrating, try living in my shoes. It's like trying to slow a runaway car with a stick.

I'm well aware of my flighty personality and inability to get to a point.

The struggle is real and not always understood. It's what makes me who I am.

Sorry, not sorry.

To the Families of My Students

Some days, I just have to stop and realize how lucky I am to have a job that is made even more fulfilling because of the support, gratitude, and laughter that is given to me by the families of my students.

You honestly don't understand how, just by being such incredible support system to your child and me on their journey to academic and personal success, I find so much daily gratitude that I get to be the one guiding them.

Your constant words of kindness, appreciation, and proactive support for your child's amazing growth mean so much more to me than just a passing conversation. I feel so blessed to be a part of your lives.

Even on the days when life is not on my side (bills, my own two babies and their love of bickering, illness, appointments, deadlines, real-life hardships), even the smallest words, actions, and achievements from your children bring a smile to my face. Without trying, their stories make me laugh every day.

I guess I just needed to express it. I tell my own family every day how super my students' families are. Just your encouragement and the ability to enjoy a laugh or an "aha" moment when your child meets a goal are so enjoyable.

You are doing such an amazing job raising some amazing children.

Never forget that!

Thank you for everything!

Under Construction

I am no longer that girl who once hid behind depression and anxiety to appease those who felt I could "get over it and just think positive." I am no longer ashamed to share my stories about the times that were so black and hopeless that I felt as though I couldn't fight the evils within my struggles any longer.

Whatever your beliefs are regarding medication for depression, anxiety, etc., I pray that you at least hear me when I say this: the right medication and the ability to open up to a therapist *literally* saved my life years ago. To think that I couldn't see past the first step in getting help, or that I possibly couldn't see the mother, daughter, friend, and advocate that I have become today is unreal to me.

Some will never know the darkness within our journeys. They are the lucky ones.

Some will refuse to believe that medication can, indeed, save a life. Those are the unfortunate ones.

Some will give the pharmaceutical route a chance—perhaps, like me, because life became a weight they could no longer carry. They will see, slowly, a mindset no longer riddled with hopelessness, a life with meaning, a life where they learn to grow stronger with every breath.

They are the fighters, fierce and damn mighty.

It's not easy, and some days I must fake a smile and persevere until the dark cloud passes.

But … it passes.

Nobody needs to suffer needlessly. You are never alone. You are not broken beyond repair.

You are not broken at all.

We are all "under construction" in one way or another, and we can be okay with ourselves.

Believe and talk about it.

I will listen.

Random Randomness, Part One, 2010

Why is it that children with the stomach bug seem to throw up in their sleep so that the washing machine gets a 3 a.m. workout and we moms get the fun job of trying to comfort and give a bath to the vomit-covered patient? Do I get a bonus in my motherhood paycheck this week?

***

Praying that my kids don't pick up the stomach bug that everyone at their daycare has gotten. I have the weakest stomach for vomit and will have to put on a strong Mommy front to comfort them while wanting to get sick from the clean up (insert me dry heaving here).

***

I was dreading the fact that I have to dress the kids up soon for their annual pic with Santa (to make my OCD calm down and have my seventh Santa pic in the series framed and in its place on the mantle). Until it dawned on me that I have very few years left in which my children still believe in him. Now I've depressed myself.

Damn you, fat man!

***

I hate when people add "eeeeee" to words like "love" on their Facebook posts. Glad you love your friends and all, but "loveeeee" annoys the crap out of "meeeeee."

***

Crayons, check ... helmet, check ... Prozac, check ... *Okay, I'm ready for work!*

***

Why is it that on weekends the kids are always up before 7 a.m., yet schoolday mornings are like performing a resurrection and exorcism both at the same time?

***

Spent the day with my children, and even though we just chillaxed around the house all day, it was so nice to have a day to just learn them a little more.

***

You know you're a mom when "no" seems to mean "please repeat the question."

***

I am starting to empathize with my children's hamster. This wheel of life is exhausting and I keep running and running, hoping it will lead me to something exciting that doesn't involve work and responsibility. I am *beat* and there is still grocery shopping and costume hunting for the perfect seven-year-old Transformer ensemble to cross off my Saturday to-do list. Who stole my f%#cking "easy" button?

***

So how is a mom supposed to respond when her son wakes up in the morning and asks why his "penis is being silly and pointing straightwards 'this big'" when he was just trying to enjoy his first pee of the morning?

***

Does it drive anyone else nuts to know that unless you do your laundry in the nude, you always have something that needs to be washed? Maybe it's just an OCD thing, but it truly drives me nuts to know that it never ends.

***

You know you find the simple things in life are wonderful when you get excited when your four-year-old daughter wakes up and tells you, "Mommy, guess what my good news is? I didn't go pee in my bed last night!"

***

I would love to know who buried me alive in a life-sized pile of bullshit. Please give me a clue as to where the shovel is to dig my way out and back to some kind of sanity.

***

I laughed when my daughter came in the room the other day wearing my push-up bra and flip-flops. But I don't know quite how to feel when my son followed suit a few minutes after her wearing a more padded, bigger plunging bra.

***

Buying my son a Nintendo DS was the equivalent decision to giving a drug addict an unlimited supply of free crack. Now he's obsessed with that evil, mind-numbing noise box. What was I thinking? Whatever happened to enjoying to good old-fashioned fresh air during childhood?

***

I pray for the ignorant people in the world who are quick to judge children with special needs because they are too uneducated to look beyond their exterior behaviors to discover the amazing little people hidden within. What a wonderful world it could be if the parents of "perfect" children could walk in the shoes of a parent with a child with special needs for one day. Perhaps their eyes could finally open to what a blessed miracle that child has brought to the world.

***

Behind every smart woman is a man that doesn't know what's going on. Sorry guys. Sometimes I gotta pay daps to all the ladies out their who feel this way but don't have the heart to carve it into your foreheads.

***

I've got ADD and OCD, so that means I've got something new to obsess about every five seconds.

***

My son woke up this morning saying, "Mommy, my underwear have been bothering me *all* night!" I checked the situation and noticed that his tightie-whities were on backwards like a thong with the pee-pee pocket on his little butt. That made my morning with a good laugh.

***

Yep folks, it's Saturday night at 9:27, and I'm already looking forward to chillin' in bed watching mindless TV. I don't know whether that's really a comforting notion … or just plain sad.

***

Dylanie did great on her first day of kindergarten, despite the fact that she colored her *entire* face with blue sidewalk chalk one minute before the bus came—all because I told her she couldn't wear makeup to kindergarten. Still, she found a way to rebel— only my daughter!

***

Actually slept past 6 a.m. on a weekend morning. Then I woke up in a panic thinking I was late for something.

***

Nothing brings me back to reality like the magic of catching fireflies for the first time last night with my kids. Logan said, "Mommy, this is why night time is magical, right?" Dylanie had a fit because she thought they could be our new pets. Such different little people!

***

Whoever said the bathroom is the only alone time you get with children apparently never had kids pounding on the door wanting in or fingers under the door.

My son passes me notes under the bathroom door when I tell him I'm refusing to talk to him until I'm out. This is in addition to incessant banging on the door, jiggling the knob, suddenly having to "go *real* bad" the second I lock the door, or (my favorite) waiting until I'm "indisposed" to beat the hell out of each other and scream like an appendage was ripped off.

The little people bearing my DNA and last name will find me even if I used the latrines in Guam. They have potty radar.

Why Share?

This morning, a friend made a comment questioning why anyone would post a picture online (Facebook in particular) of a child with a deformity, mental illness, and the like. While I respect that everyone has his or her own views, I felt that I needed to give insight on my own perception about this subject.

Here was my answer: Maybe the families of what this friend called, those "kids with health problems and deformities" aren't simply looking for a "like." Maybe they are proud to share their child with the world or to help raise awareness that not every child is born, externally or internally, from society's perfect prototypical mold. Or perhaps they post such pictures so that the people in the world that find them upsetting or "sad" will maybe gain greater insight, empathy, or even acceptance to a world that is so lacking in a need for awareness when it comes to individuals with special needs.

True, there are a lot of questionable people in the world that will use social media as their own popularity playground for recognition and faux friendships/fans. But try to remember that there are still an astronomical growing number of families in our world who are reaching out to the population (sadly, technology has made actual interpersonal relationships and advocacy almost null and void) to give these children a voice or an existence within this distorted, unrealistic, "Stepford-perfect" world that has so brutally pushed physical and intellectual perfection to be what really matters.

And yet, not to minimize people's emotions when these photos surface, sometimes it is heart wrenching to see an innocent creature who wasn't as blessed as many of us. It's okay to feel a surge of anguish or inner-pain to see another human struggling to live their lives in a body or mind that takes longer, more painstaking, grueling paths to get to the daily destinies we visit without a second thought and without the gratitude that we should have for the ease with which we our said paths.

We are all somebody's child, in one way or another. Like many others, I am one of those lucky ones who has a family that cheered me higher when I succeeded and supported me during times I was at my lowest. And at my lowest—and I've been pretty low—my family showed me just *that much more* how much they believed in me and what I was capable of in terms of being the best *me* I could achieve and share with the world around me. If my lowest, most emotionally torn moments were captured in snapshots (as dark and scary as I may have portrayed myself), I know my mother would have seen through the unsettling image and kept right on as my biggest cheerleader. At my worst, my mother reminds me and the world around me of my best.

Think about your own personal rock-bottom moment, if you will, where the future looked bleak, unattainable, hopeless … *sad*. Most likely, it was a moment that, if somehow captured in a photograph and shown to a stranger (one whose life fell into that earlier mentioned "perfect prototype"), that photo would have ignited ignorance, judgment, and misunderstanding toward you (just a "sad" image captured in a shutter frame). To each and every stranger who glanced at this photo, this painful memory passed, a different opinion might be made: positive, negative, empathetic, blaming.

The point is, at your lowest emotional/physical breaking point, someone in your life knew the person in that photo—yet knew them outside the photo so much more in beautiful depth.

They saw past the vision that probably would invoke an internal dark judgment from someone who never stepped outside their perfectly sheltered world to stand for a moment in a life they didn't live. A life that is *really easy* to scroll past when it surfaces on our comfortable social media pages because we don't want to deal with having to imagine such a struggle.

When you have a child—regardless of the why's, how's, what if's, where's, and how's—you accept, love, cherish, hope, and *believe*. I've learned that, while it certainly didn't take an entire village to help me in my journey as a mother, it took enough people in my "village" to really open my eyes and mind to see *all* the beauty that only children can bring to the world. To find gratitude in the successes that come easily for some children and not others. To accept that some days aren't going to be as pretty as the planned idea, but nonetheless, life tends to laugh at our idealistic "pretty" dreams one moment, and rewards us with Popsicle stick art and sticky kisses the next.

Please remember something I learned in my own journey: We fortunate ones may be able bodied and of sound mind—at this moment.

Don't scroll through so fast. You are missing someone's miracle.

I *"like"* this!"

Please Remind Me

There are moments as a parent that make the times I want to commit myself to the loony bin so worth the craziness.

Last night, my little girl asked my permission to grow her hair long so that she could have it cut off and donate it to people with cancer who needed it more than she does. She told me she had learned about "Locks of Love" and that she wanted my permission to donate her own hair.

I was so taken back with pride. I explained that if she wanted to donate her hair, they would have to cut it very short to meet the minimum required length for donation. She told me that she didn't care about giving it away and having her hair cut short because it would grow back someday, and her hair would go to someone who really needed it.

From every moment I have worked to guide my children and model the right behaviors, I have never been so moved by a choice that was made by my child—a choice that I had *no* role in. A selfless idea that somehow came about as simply the right thing to do for another human being—and one that didn't result in an award or extra allowance money.

Can someone please remind me of this day down the road when I am feeling that impending wave of failure as a parent to my children?

Remind me that I somehow did something so right by my child. In some way, she has learned, in her own way, what truly makes the world a beautiful place.

Like a Rock

In the most metaphorical, abstract ways to view the paths in which our lives take—I choose to think of about rocks along the shoreline.

Rocks, like humans, begin their journeys believing that they know their destiny and place in the universe. Smooth or rough, new and unknowing of future fate, unique and strong in their own ways.

Just a mere part of this universe, thinking it will endure its existence as a rock. Unscathed and strong.

Like humans, the rock is jaded and ignorant. Life, for most, becomes a vortex of unexpected circumstances and cruel realities. The tides are not always calm, the atmosphere and weather are not kind. The environment surrounding their simplistic existences begins many journeys that decide their fate.

Like humans, the rocks on the shoreline fall victim to life on life's terms. Whether it's the weight of a human's careless step, the unpredicted passing storm bringing devastation, the reality of years passing and wearing down what was once so strong—the rock breaks down.

The rock changes, tries to adapt to its new form. Perhaps life has turned its existence into a smaller, weaker, more jagged form than it had known before. Perhaps its appearance isn't as desirable as it was before it endured the change. Maybe it fell to the ground, now residing in a place foreign and vulnerable compared with where it had always known.

It still remains a rock.

And although, like humans, the rock might believe that the worst had taken over its role as a rock in the universe—when it has learned to accept and believe that the stormy times had passed and life would remain status quo, the waves rise up and pull it from the comforts of the shoreline into an ocean of unknown fate.

Random Randomness, Part Two, 2011

Feeling oddly grateful to hear my kids constant bickering and tattles. It means I am lucky to have healthy children who are safe and unbelievably loved. I pray for those parents who would give anything to have what I have in my life.

***

Keep smacking your food while you eat ... watch me break out my ninja skills

***

Logan: "Mommy, do dogs and cats dream?"
Me: "I'm sure they do."
Logan (pondering this): "Well then what about vegetarians?"

Even with the gratitude for all the treasures in my little world, why can't I muster the ability to find peace with the anxious demons inside me that squelch my need to just relax and feel happiness? Do I even *own* a happy place?

***

Lanie (sneaky, on the phone with operator from a toy commercial): "Hi, this is Dylanie Muller and, um, I want that thing on the TV so can you please send it to me now?"

Operator: "You are such a little sweetheart. Have a nice day honey."

Dylanie: "Okay. So you send it now, and I will watch out my window for the toy truck."

Two hours later: five-year old girl still pressed against the window and angry with the truck's no-show.

***

Kids fed, bathed, teeth brushed, kisses given ... I'm a millionaire!

***

Nothing paints a Norman Rockwell-like scene like a home-cooked chicken dinner, my family sitting around the table eating, and my daughter teaching us about the newest addition to her vocabulary: "buttcrack."

***

3:45 a.m.: "Mommy, is it morning enough yet to get up?"

***

Sometimes I wonder what the meaning to life really is. And then I look at my children and realize the answer is right before me. They keep me strong somehow when I struggle to put one foot in front of the other.

***

Cleaning my house today with hyper kids is the equivalent of shovelling during an avalanche. I am throwing in the towel. I officially have a kid-infested home.

***

Every Trisha Muller Mommy Doll comes complete with selectively deaf children, gray hair, and no adult time to talk on the phone, pee without child interruption, and half-shaved legs. Some features sold separately, including Prozac, Debt Statement, Psychotherapist Chair, and Overflowing Swear Jar. Batteries not included.

***

In the serene quiet sanctum of this blessed Saturday morning lurks the evil haze of the impending bickering and tattling from my kids just frantic to fog my home with it's deadly abilities to awaken the "Screaming Demonic Mommy Syndrome" I keep squelched behind my June Cleaver disguise.

***

One day the house will be clean, nothing will be broken, no one running around. It will be quiet … and I'll miss all of it.

***

Me: "Dylanie, have you been behaving for Daddy today?"

Dylanie: "I was a little fresh Mama. I tried and tried and tried to behave, but it was too hard for me."

Me: "Well, you need to behave for Father's Day."

Dylanie: "But Logan poured a pail of sand down my underwear first!"

***

While Lanie was rubbing my back last night, she got this horrified look on her face when she realized I had nothing on under my T-shirt. She then proceeded to ask me that since my "grown up lady boobie thing" (a bra, for those clueless) wasn't on, had I "forgotten to where my boobies today." I love her little inquiring mind

But I'm also very, very afraid. Dylanie is going to be six in less than a month—six going on twenty-six and already wants to know when she can start wearing a "big boobie under the shirt thing like grown up ladies." Get my padded room and shackles ready for when I go loony tunes in a few years.

***

I *hate* seeing my babies sick. I don't care how old they are. I still go into Mommy Mode to comfort them. I will be stalking them in college when they have the sniffles. Just hope I don't catch it. The Mom career doesn't allow for sickness or time off from our duties.

***

Dylanie: "Mommy, I don't want to get bigger because I don't want you to leave and go to heaven like Bambi's Mommy."

Me (teary-eyed): "Lanie, Mommy will always take care of you because that's the job God gave us."

Dylanie: "Will you still cook macaroni and cheese when you're an angel in Heaven?"

Me (no words … just tight hugs).

***

So I bought a lampshade for my bedroom lamp the other day. My daughter spies it in my car and asks if it's for her dog to wear around her neck, "so that she can't lick her privates anymore." Then, as if that little moment wasn't all telling enough about my children, I find my son in his room with the new lampshade on his head while he's playing his DS and laughing himself sick. I'm just so proud.

***

I will blame my haggard, beat-down appearance today on the rain and *not* my blubbering self when I get to work after my babies leave my side and go off to school today. Maybe if I get in Lanie's line with my name tag, they will mistake me for a 5'2" first-grader. It's worth a shot.

***

My daughter asked me why grown-ups never cry. I told her that everybody cries when they need to. She responded that she never saw me crying. If only our children knew how raw and emotional we really were when they were in the other room in all their innocence.

***

Grateful for the negative people/issues in my life that made me move forward and find better, more positive paths toward happiness and success. Thank you so much for showing me the type of person/life I never want to be remembered for.

***

Really? Awake before 3 a.m. *every* weekday morning? This is starting to wear thin. Good thing I'm such a warm ray of sunshine by nature in the morning (insert sarcasm and growling).

***

I remember when I was little, I used to wonder why we couldn't afford the things I asked for. My mom promised me I would get what I wanted when "her ship came in." Well, I'm now thirty-four and starting to wonder where the hell this damn mystery money boat is. Hell, I'd settle for a dingy right about now.

***

I knew I had succeeded as a mom when, after winning enough tickets at Nomads to get herself a decent sized prize, the first thing my little girl told the lady at the prize counter was she, "had to pick something out for her brother" because he didn't get to go to the party. I went right somewhere with my kids ... so blessed.

***

Positive conferences for both kids ... both doing great academically. Now if only Dylanie would stop being such a mischievous chatterbox diva in class. History is repeating itself. Now I feel for my Mom having to go to my old elementary conferences.

***

Not gonna lie. I sometimes giggle when the ketchup bottle makes a fart noise. So I guess my kids are a chip off my unique block.

Snitches

Dylanie has been on a new kick lately. As many if you know, it's *truly* a crapshoot as to what is going to roll out of my daughter's mouth.

Like her mother, yours truly, her thought-to-verbalization process is too often full of unfiltered, colorful, and outlandish moments that have the power to stop a whirling dervish dead in her tracks.

It's a beautiful, innate gift we share together: the ability to see the forest for the trees and yet not feel apologetic when we address the bear shitting in the woods.

That being said … she has become incessant about wanting me to have another baby. No clue what sparked the idea (an idea that makes my uterus duck and cover somewhere behind my vital organs). Maybe it's some newfound maternal desire she has developed, maybe she's grown bored of humiliating the household felines in old doll attire and rainbow loom accessories.

Who knows? All I am aware of is the fact that she's made this wish on dandelion puffs and fallen eyelashes. Many times. (Knowing Lanie, she's probably manually removed a stray cat's whisker or two to wish on for good measure.)

I needed to finally squelch her pipe dreams in the only way that seemed fitting. In our household, we have learned that honesty is the only remedy for addressing the head-scratching ponders that constantly spew from the mouths of my children.

I simply told her that I loved my little family the way it was and that I wouldn't be having any more children. The doctors made sure that my family would be complete and full of love and eternal devotion.

And in her own, beautifully unique perspective, she finally understood.

"So the doctor gave you "snitches" (stitches) like they gave to Charolette?"

Charolette is our black lab.

Whelp …

"Exactly! The doctor gave mom stitches so I could give all my love to you and your brother!"

"Awww!! Way to ruin my plans Mom!"

All I can picture in my mind is my daughter's disappointment in me—and her visual of me with a cone around my neck.

And *that,* my friends, concludes my weekend contribution to a "moment in the life of the Muller world."

Now back to your regularly scheduled sanity.

More Gratitude

What is gratitude?

My house is a constant disaster, but I have a warm dwelling and can afford a mortgage.

My son is autistic and my daughter is becoming a preteen with an attitude. However, my children are not missing or terminally ill. I can still tuck them in every night.

Regarding my son's diagnosis—it's a struggle I never intended and a huge struggle at that. Yet I am formally educated and headstrong enough to fight tooth and nail to ensure he will always be given every opportunity he deserves.

My family is small and we've seen the hell that arose from my dad's stroke and stole far too many aspects of his life. My brother has special needs. We get sad a lot and isolated. But we've got each other's backs and have learned to laugh and make the best of what God thought we needed.

I am extremely educated, with student loans up the wazoo, but I choose to work in a field that brings me joy everyday, regardless of the income. True, I could make so much more doing something that feels like work. I chose pride, love, and sheer pleasure in where I landed.

Yes, I could be better off financially. But my bills are always paid and I have all that I need.

My wardrobe could be so much bigger. I have found myself complaining that I have nothing to wear. However, I am never without clothes on my back, nor are my children. Labels and trends are only "in" for so long.

We don't always have a fridge stocked with something to appease everyone's appetite. Yet, we never, ever go hungry.

The miles are getting up there on my vehicle. The fact that I own a car without a payment is a blessing.

It took thirty-seven years to come to a point where I can honestly find peace in the simple, beautiful life I have achieved.

The Po-Po

Driving home from our friend's house last evening, we happened to be approaching a vehicle pulled over by a cruiser in the distance.

My nine-year-old, little brown-eyed princess proceeded to pipe up from the backseat, "Uh oh, Mom. Better watch your speed. There's Po-Po up ahead!"

"Dylanie, you really need to not speak like that. It makes you sound ignorant. Where did you even hear that term?"

Sometimes I curse myself in mid-sentence. I am better off ignoring the comments and redirecting her attention to, let's say, I don't know, counting how many blue cars we see on the ride home. But *no!* I went *there.* I fell right into the trap that has abducted my sweet little girl and replaced her with a sassy teenager disguised as a fourth grader.

"Umm … duh, Mom! Don't you know how kids talk? Everyone knows that the police are called the Po-Po. Even though we look like twins and my friends think you're pretty, there's a lot of things you aren't understanding!"

Verbatim as always.

She does have a valid point. I could write a book about simply not understanding how to "learn" this obscure, new female who is trying too hard to not be a child.

Stay young a little longer, child! This adult thing sucks!

Don't Look Back

What's on my mind?

The fact that I just spent a half an hour obsessively trying to find out the source of a foul smell that was following me everywhere.

Without going into too much detail, let's just say that I have literally sniffed every square inch of myself and the inside of my car (picture a bloodhound in a crime scene) wondering what in God's name stanks like the ass of Lucifer after he ate tainted Thai cuisine.

As I was about to give up and hang my head in shame with the acceptance that I was simply gross and rotting with gangrene in an unknown place, I realized that every time I turned my head to look for the retched smell it seemed to permeate from behind me.

I never thought to remove my jacket and sniff the back of it. It's not something I do on a regular basis. Perhaps I should make it part of my routine from here on in when I smell a dead water buffalo within my vicinity.

Yep. One of the cats must have gotten pissed at their cuisine yesterday and retaliated by taking a whiz and on the back of my jacket.

Happy hump-day to me. What a pisser of the morning.

My Question Is

I was sick in bed with a stomach bug and I still had to make sure the kids were taken care of. I made lunches and, of course, both kids wanted different things. He wanted a sandwich, and she wanted waffles. I figured that was easy enough. He ate his lunch without complaints. She whined and whined that hers was not hot enough. Being somewhat patient, I nuked it for fifteen seconds. She whined that it was too stale tasting. I told her to throw it away and make her own lunch and I'm not her maid. She came back to my room with a giant grinder roll and asked if she could have it for lunch. Ya know what? Go for it, Lanie. Eat the darn starch ball. I didn't care at that point.

Then I remembered I have to drag my suffering ass with the kids to get Logan's hair cut for school pics this week. Right then, I would rather have had a root canal in Zimbabwe, but I have to make sure he's looking his best. I can't go tomorrow because I have a friend's baby shower to attend. So I forced myself to get out and get it over with. Lanie started whining that she never gets a haircut and I'm not fair. So I fixed the problem by telling her I was bringing her too to get a Mohawk

So my question is, am I still an okay mother or have I solidified therapy for my daughter someday?

Me Time

I adore my kids. But I can't always be Supermom.

"Certain people" will disagree with me, but I am really at a saturation point. Brownies, Cub Scout fundraisers, CCD, school functions, PPTs, etc. and I *never* get a non-work/school night or full weekend to do anything adult related. I am made to feel guilty for feeling this way and I *know* my kids will remember all I did and tried to do for them someday. I just sometimes feel like I need a reason to look forward to … something just for me.

I have been told numerous times by "certain people" that, "that's what Moms do." Really!? What then is the goal for me to work my ass off every day of my life? Watching others have their time off to enjoy themselves while I do, "what Moms do"?

It's hard for me to go into detail because I don't want to air my dirty laundry (Ha! Isn't that what Facebook is for?) However, my custody agreement hasn't been changed in years, and sometimes "me time" is not feasible in terms of having something as small as an entire weekend to myself.

Then there is the fact that I am riddled with guilt for wanting just a little time away. I just need to believe that I am more than someone who takes care of everyone else. It seems to be my way of life.

Random Randomness, Part Three, 2012

Mandatory TMI posting: The idea of possibly not being able to shower for any amount of time has forced me to indulge in shaving the way I was only able to do before kids. Club Med be damned. This girl feels pampered.

Yes, I'm a pathetic individual. Take pity on me.

***

Lately I've realized how much I wish I could be a child again. My world was so full of love and peace of mind. This adult thing really sucks sometimes.

***

All I'm asking for is a less insane day than yesterday. You will know if this wish is not granted when my new profile pic shows me in the corner of a padded room rocking and drooling on myself with a vest around me that lets me hug myself and is adorned with industrial-strength shiny buckles.

***

I hate that in order to survive I have to work and not see my kids as often as I'd like. I hate that when I'm not working, I have to do so many required grown-up tasks that I don't have time for my family and friends. You guys are my life, and I feel like by earning a living, I am missing who makes my life livable. Stupid emotions!

***

I love how some people are complaining that they prepared for nothing with this latest winter storm that didn't fully materialize. After last October being unprepared, freezing, no food, no showers, no extra batteries or flashlights, no generator, and no power for nine full days—I am glad I was prepared for the worst-case scenario this time. The gas, food, water, and other supplies that we bought can be used anyway. The same people who are complaining about all the hype from this storm would have been the same complaining and blaming the news and utility companies/workers if they had been hit with any devastation or power outages. Just be grateful if you made it out of this storm with your family, health, and little catastrophe. I certainly am.

***

Dylanie quote of the day: "When I have to use the bathroom, I pretend I'm a bus. When I pee. It's like I'm letting the kids off, then I wash my hands and pretend I'm washing the bus because, you know, kids get their germs everywhere with their dirty hands and bubble gum blowing."

I swear I am not making this up. My daughter amuses, amazes, and exhausts me.

***

My daughter's random thoughts frighten and exhaust me when she verbalizes them: "When I'm a Mommy, I'm gonna buy a kangaroo suit and carry my babies in my pouch. That way I can hop around wherever I need to go and sweat too, because fur makes you sweaty sometimes."

***

True story: While checking my groceries out in Stop & Shop today, the cashier insisted on explaining to me how her ultimate Valentine's gift would be a life-sized mannequin of Michael Jackson. It never fails. Awkward people are drawn to me.

***

To Whom it May Concern:
If your child is vomiting, has diarrhea, a fever, sore throat, pink eye, or is excessively runny from any bodily area—please do not try to mask their ailment with over-the-counter meds and send them out. They should be home in their own bed getting better and not infecting *everyone* around them. My kids and I would appreciate not inheriting the sicknesses of every ill child who should have stayed home.
Thank you for your future cooperation.

***

Only in my world would I have to threaten to turn the car around and cancel our much-awaited trip to visit a friend in New York because there was a heated argument between my kids over "who farted?"

***

I amuse myself looking at profile photos of females who take daily pics of themselves posing with their camera phones and making that ridiculous face that I'm assuming they think is sexy. I especially love how sexy the pics are when taken in the bathroom. Nothing screams seduction like the family crapper in the background.

***

No ... really ... I got it ... just let me activate my five sets of arms and legs ... you just keep doing a great job of what it is you're doing ... it's all good.

***

I'm supposed to be tackling laundry, but reruns of *Cops* get me every time. At this rate, I will be wearing the hamper to work if I don't wash my clothes. But there are laws about public nudity, so I had better get to it.

***

What is up with that retched smell coming from the local fields? I understand that they need to fertilize, but do they need to use the manure from cows that obviously indulged in some tainted Thai food? I nearly threw up in my lap this morning when I drove through.

***

Don't get me started on the conversation I had with Lanie that summed up every topic ranging from when she could get a real tattoo, when she would have "big circle boobies," how doctors get babies out and why it hurts, and how I wasn't a regular mommy because I'm too short.

***

Welcome to my life—only in my existence could we have had four of the Mega Millions winning numbers in *sequential order* and walked away with a hearty, affluent $7! So for all those who I promised to share the wealth with after I hit big … let me know if you want your 19 cents in cash or check.

***

FYI: I suck at Dance Dance Revolution. Let's leave it at that

***

I must love my Dad. He always insists I make deviled eggs for holiday gatherings and I came through like always. Unfortunately, my cute little house now reeks like a gargantuous egg fart.

***

My little boy picked me a bouquet of violets from the backyard because he knew purple was my favorite color. He's my favorite boy in the world, hands down.

***

Why do some elderly people feel it is an acceptable practice to openly and repeatedly blow their nose in the middle of a crowded restaurant where people are paying good money to enjoy their meals? Is it that absurd to ask that they spread their disgusting germs and ignorance inside those great inventions called "restrooms"? I almost had to ask for a side of Lysol and a smallpox vaccination with my meal. Next time it happens, I'm going to take a seat beside the perpetrators, prop my bare feet next to their plate, and play footsie with their fork.

***

Awake ungodly early, worked 8:30 to 5:30, raced to Lanie's soccer practice, kid's doctor's appointment at 7 p.m., flew home to give baths, got kiddos ready for bed, and packed lunches for tomorrow. At some point, I managed to eat supper and am now paralyzed with exhaustion. I'm sexy and I know it.

***

Can someone recommend a forum for my family (mostly targeting the males, big and small) that focuses on shutting off the lights when leaving the room, the knowledge that when the toilet paper roll is finished the new roll does not magically levitate and attach itself to the dispenser, clothes do not grow legs and travel from the bedroom floor where they were thrown and catapult themselves into that mind-boggling device known as a "clothes hamper," and that they will not self-destruct if (a) they actually pee into the giant opening on the toilet and not the surrounding bathroom landscape and (b) as much as I love seeing the finished product(s) upon bathroom productivity, that shiny knob on the side of the toilet is not a detonation device and can be pulled upon completion?

Am I asking to find Atlantis here? And don't get me started on that state-of-the-art product of the new millennium called a "dishwasher" conveniently located next to the sink that appears to be a head-scratcher for those household members to exert themselves enough place their dirty dishes in.

All input will be gratefully appreciated.

***

Today has been brought to us by the letters W, T, and F.

—

Logan: "Hey Mom, what does "WTF" stand for?"
Me: "Ummmm ... It means, "wow that's fabulous."
I'm in trouble.

***

Setting: Stop and Shop grocery store.
Dylanie: "Can we go see the lobsters?"
Me: "Of course."
Dylanie: "I want to find the King Lobster!"
Setting: Lobster tank, nearly empty except for two lobsters in the corner having what certainly looked like lobster "afternoon delight."
Me: (silent panicking)
Dylanie (top volume, of course): "Oh my God, Mommy, look what that lobster is doing to he other one! He must be the King!"
Conclusion: Customers snickering. Me rolling my cart at nano speed and telling Lanie we need to find the bagel aisle.
Could I make his up!?

***

All kidding aside, if you really had three wishes granted that would make your lives more peaceful and fulfilling, what would they be? I would take away the hardships in my mom's world (although that may count as a few wishes), would give my children the self-confidence it would take to allow them to be strong, successful individuals in a cruel world, and grant myself just enough financial security to live my life without worrying about the fact that I *can't* live life because I need to work my days away to get by or constantly go without because I *can't* afford to indulge. Not too much to ask if I was truly offered three wishes, right?

***

Hate that my little girl is sick, but I'm *so* happy to have had a chance to take a day and just soak her in. She makes my heart happy with her witty ways. Wish I could stop time. My children complete me in every way a Mom should be completed. Never take even the littlest moment for granted. Blink and they have grown. Love you to the moon and back Logan and Dylanie … someday you will understand that you will always be my miracles!

***

Dear obnoxious, rude woman at the Dollar Tree,

Just wanted to express my understanding of your ignorance whereas you didn't see it at all in good nature to let me go ahead of you in line with my three items while you rang up an $83 purchase and talked on your phone the entire time. I'm certain the insane amount of worthless treasures you bought while not paying attention to your screaming toddler was definitely more pressing than my wasted lunch break. May we only be so blessed as to meet again like today. After all, who *doesn't* need enough Rice Crispy Treats to feed a third world country?

Regards,

Trisha

PS. I hope your snacks are stale and you chip a tooth.

***

Just wanted to thank the multitude of people on the Shaker Road soccer field Saturday morning who witnessed a man take a fall and never so much as offered to help him up or ask if he was okay. Maybe the cane he uses to walk wasn't enough of a hint for all of you that he has trouble walking. By all means, it made much more sense to stand there and watch him struggle than to offer a helping hand. I'm thanking you because, as someone put it to me today, your lack of compassion makes me proud to a better human being than you. Hope you never have to walk in another person's struggling shoes. You may just find that ignorant morons like yourself would rather turn a blind eye than offer a big heart

***

Headed to orthopedic doctor for follow-up. Only I could break my foot on Mother's Day going to get a pedicure. I should just live in a mile thick layer of bubble wrap. On the plus side, my toes look spectacular even if it appears a purple elbow is growing out of the side of my swollen foot. FYI: trying to suck it up to get a pedicure immediately following busting up your foot is not advised and *not* a relaxing experience.

***

It's called "personal space" for a reason. When I can feel the fibers of your nose hair and keeping moving away from you, that is your clue that your "person" is within my kicking space. Don't make me cause you to wish you weren't so darn close.

***

Only at my house on a sunny Sunday afternoon would I hear my little girl screaming in the pool for all the neighbors to hear: "Logan! You just kicked me in the balls!"

***

Is it better to tell the kids the truth about their kitty, or do I make up a story about him running away? I'm so torn.

***

So last night, while driving to get my kids a Friday night Happy Meal, my nine-year-old son asked me if he has "swagger."

I come deathly close to driving off the road. Perhaps I need to monitor their choices in music and TV a tad better.

***

My exhaust pipe literally is falling off of my car and it sounds like I modified it to sound like something out of *The Fast and Furious*. So embarrassing. There's no sneaking up on anyone when I roll into anywhere in my little whip. Getting it fixed ASAP. People thought I was trying to race them when I was driving home from work last night.

Perfectly Imperfect

As a child, vacations on the beach were about exploring for critters, sandy hotdogs, the mesmerizing smell of Coppertone on my skin, and making impromptu friendships that lasted the duration of my stay but were forgotten weeks later.

As an adult, I yearn for my yearly vacations to the beach as time away with my children. I know their adolescent years are waiting around the corner to swoop away my "cool mom" status and replace it with the maternal nuisance figure who bitches about the importance of SPF, refuses their demands for curfews far too late for their own good, and causes bored faces screaming a longing to be with the likes of Jack The Ripper over the company of their own family.

I'm a simple, yet complex human, perfectly imperfect, emotional to a fault, and often so needlessly anxiety-ridden that I could be likened to a neurotic poodle (only I haven't started piddling on the family carpet … yet). I worry about the known and unknown, project the worst-case scenarios when problem solving in the present, incessantly find the need to please those around me—even if it means my own dismay.

But, in the most condensed way of expressing it, I worry about my children. Will my daughter make good choices as she grows into a young woman who is terrifyingly becoming the likeness of me during my adolescent years? That was an era when my parents probably pondered whether or not they would be shunned and escorted away by armed militia while trying to convince the nuns that I would make a decent addition to their convent.

And I've ached inside, in a place that I can't give a physiological name to when I think about my son, about how kind his soul is and how he doesn't understand how capable he is to succeed. Will he have the strength we've tried to instill in him to handle the hurdles before him? Will he stand up to the ignorant assholes he is certain to encounter and hold his head up high when his heart is hurting and his soul wants to cry?

And that's just who I am, how I am made to be. No apologies. Just accept it.

Accept it because, every once in a while, moments happen that give the trials and fears we all experience a swift kick in the negative ass.

Such was a moment yesterday. My daughter can walk into a barren cave and come out with an abundance of new friends, but my son often chooses his own solitary company. On rare occasions, he will branch out to others his age in hopes that they might share his same interests. During those times, I watch from a distance with pride and anguish, praying that his acquaintances see him for all that he is—praying that I don't have to step in and put the fear of God into anyone who doesn't.

My son hit me yesterday. Hard.

Figuratively of course, but, nonetheless, hit me with a blow I needed. If there is such a quadrant in the body that holds the painful apprehension organs within a special needs mother, my little man struck it with such force that the wind was knocked out of me.

We were seated on the beach parallel to a family with younger children. I was close enough to hear their conversations. They were speaking French, so I hadn't a clue as to what they spoke of.

After a few minutes, I saw Logan at the water's edge, taking in the waves. As I opened my mouth to ask if he wanted my company, it happened.

"Mom, is it okay if I ask those kids next to us if they want to play with me?"

No, the hit was still in the works. My quadrant was exposed, unknowing that it was about to be struck with such force, such beauty, such knowledge from the child I thought I had taught about the world.

"Logan, that's a sweet idea, but those children don't speak English. I'm not sure they will understand what you want."

He didn't skip a beat, never paused to internalize my rationalization. Instead, he came back swinging.

"Mom, who cares if they don't speak English? I just want to be their friend. We can still be friends and hang out. They don't have to speak the same language to be my friend!"

And just like that, I felt something indescribable leave my body as I exhaled. All those years of college, training, studying, fighting, crying, wanting to give in, wanting to give up, asking why, feeling sorry, feeling angry, feeling envy …

Gone.

Even if only for the moment. It was a moment I will cherish. He gave me the gift of a moment that made me realize something I needed to know.

I am winning.

We are winning.

I am learning with him, and we are going to be okay.

We Remember

The same, sweet elderly couple keeps finding us to converse with on the beach.

He's an encyclopedia of knowledge with Sean about his days as a fisherman.

She's a fragile vortex of memories that she can't seem to make verbal.

She wanted so badly to express in words how much I reminded her of herself in her youth, searching the ocean's tide for treasurers. Yet her words came forth jumbled, trapped in a memory that couldn't find its verbal path to share with me as she remembered.

And it was okay. We spoke in short, near-aphasic prose, in a way that she believed I could see her past, young and carefree. Finding the magic of the ocean, unknowing of her future self, a self that knows what I know: that the ocean creates memories, whether we want them or not.

I laughed with her broken words and smiled. And, somehow, she believed I heard her, understood her.

And I did.

Her husband, frail and determined, took her hand.

His eyes met mine in gratitude for giving her a gift, though theatric. For helping her believe that I understood her memories, be them real or imagined. For helping her smile.

And every time they pass by, he takes her hand. He keeps her close. He remembers too, that woman she speaks of in broken verses.

And they walk away.

How beautiful, her hand in his as they walk away.

Ten Randoms

Here are ten randoms, in random order:

1. I am shamefully passive-aggressive and will please others just to avoid drama.

2. I had two awful pregnancies and hated every second of them. Especially since my daughter was almost born at twenty-one weeks.

3. I am obsessed with my teeth and have nightmares about them falling out.

4. I am so turned off by people with bad breath that I will either avoid them or frantically try to preach oral hygiene perks and gum.

5. I was diagnosed in 1996 with depression and anxiety and deal every day with the crippling effects.

6. I love tattoos and my mother hates them. I got my first at eighteen and didn't tell her about it until I was twenty-four. It's an unspoken issue between us that I have many more. I would get inked so much more if I had the money. I would get them where my mother didn't have to see them.

7. I can't say "I love you" easily to family. I don't know why because my family is everything. Saying it feels like being nude in public to me. I love my family and want nothing but peace for them.

8. I will always laugh at a fart. Even if the situation is inappropriate to laugh. The more inappropriate, the funnier it is.

9. If I could have any career in the world, my ideal life path would be to become an advocate for families with children who have autism. It is an obsession of mine to spread awareness to the beautiful, unique world of the "spectrum."

10. I have a tail. Like an actual tail, as my tailbone protrudes a good inch and a half from my bony behind.

Eat Up, Beautiful

So, I'm having this dream that I'm in a quaint little 50s-era-type diner. I'm seated in a booth face to face with Channing Tatum, and he refuses to break his stare from my eyes. After professing his undying attraction (attraction that has stemmed within him for years), he orders me a hot fudge and peanut butter sundae big enough to park a Winnebago on.

He softly whispers to me, his eyes never leaving mine, "Eat up, beautiful. I love the way you can eat like a horse. I love your never-ending collection of yoga pants and leggings. I want you to be full so that we can show this diner and its patrons the "Pony" scene from *Magic Mike*. I'm going to need you to order some fries to go with that sundae."

The song begins to play somewhere from the kitchen as he takes my hand. My heart left my chest and found its way into my throat. I can't be too sure, but knowing me, I was probably torn between wanting him to pull his sexiest moves out on me to the beat—and wondering where my fries were.

Yet, I will never know how my dream concludes. The background music from Ginuwine's "Pony" meshed with my effing alarm clock and its asshole braying of *"ree! ree! ree!"* to rip me out of my love affair in that quaint setting. Literally and figuratively, my dream dispersed from my grasp, causing an anguish that can't be put into literary form.

As if that wasn't a rude enough way to tear my fantasy into a vortex of realities, I immediately stepped in cat vomit with my bare foot as I made my shuffle (in my yoga pants) down the hallway to start my day at 4:30 a.m.

Asshole cats.

Asshole alarm clock.

You are all very welcome. Stop laughing.

Sunday Blessing

Sometimes I just have to rejoice and find serenity and happiness in the little things.

Last night was a tough night for many reasons. Dylanie was sick and Logan was just having a rough night.

It was one of those times when a parent questions if this is truly as good as it gets.

But being awakened on a Sunday morning (which normally would have put me into a nasty mood) was such a sweet, tiny experience that made last night just a faded memory.

My son's whisper, as he peeked at my slumbering, buried face under the covers inquired if it was okay for him to bring his sister breakfast in bed because she was sick.

Just because.

It wasn't something he was offering so that he could get a reward in return.

Just because he cares about his little sister.

Because he's Logan. He's my kid and his heart is bigger than I sometimes give him credit for.

Just because I need these moments to remind me that I should slow down and notice that when I feel like I've failed or that my world is sometimes a heavy struggle, I'm the mother of the two miracles who make me whole.

Yes, it was only a box of cereal delivered from my son to his little sister in bed.

But I pushed back the covers, opened my eyes, and started my Sunday with happiness in my heart.

Just because my little man showed me another reason to celebrate every waking moment with them.

After

I can feel the emotions bubbling to the surface.

The end of our vacation always hurts me in a place so deep and indescribable.

What I wouldn't do for one more week with them.

If I leave tomorrow, they will keep growing up, growing away from those sandy little footprints on the shoreline.

Growing further from who they are when we are here, mere steps from the ocean. Simple, creative, loud, messy, needy, loving, defiant, giving, sun kissed, deep in sweet slumber together as I watch from their door.

Here, they are still everything magical that becomes an abundance of sweet childhood memories from a time so simple by the sea.

I pray they look back on these memories and see what I see: a block of their lives, reserved for us, to learn, laugh, and appreciate the gift of just being us, a family.

Time feels stolen, as though fast-forwarded like the perfect dream in slumber that the morning alarm snatches too soon. You want more, but the time has come for the reality of life.

What I wouldn't give for one more week.

What I wouldn't give to stop time so they never grow so old that they don't see my tears each year as we leave.

Stay little. Stay magic.

For me.

Does anyone else ever experience torturous sadness when arriving home after a vacation?

I swear, I can't find my motivation today or any sense of tranquility.

Is it possible to detox from the scent of salt air and the constant comfort that the sound of waves crashing provides?

If they made canned ocean air, I'm pretty confident I would be in a corner huffing it like a profound ocean addict.

I can't be alone in this. Anyone understand?

Home sweet home—what an oxymoron after coming back from paradise.

It didn't help that we had to pull over so that Logan could hurl in someone's front yard.

It didn't help that Dylanie sobbed while covering her ears as he hurled.

And the fact that one of our cats thought it would be great fun and punishment to us for leaving them that they shit and pissed from stem to stern in our main bathroom.

Excuse me while I attempt to come down from the high I received from the lethal amount of bleach I needed to clean the shitstorm (literally) I came home to.

Yup, we're home.

Birthday Treats

Days like today honestly make me realize that I have some pretty awesome people in my life, and a job that is incredible, even on the challenging days!

Thank you all first and foremost for the online birthday wishes. You are *all* so important to my world. I feel humbled.

I came to work and was greeted with birthday wishes from our littles in full volume. They gave me homemade cards with their beautiful artwork and signatures—-which not long ago they couldn't do (so proud of them!) One of my families brought me in a box of birthday munchkins (which, of course I shared with my work munchkins!).

My work family presented me with a card and gift certificate for Bertucci's, and not long after, I received an amazing delivery from Edible Arrangements with beautiful fruit flowers (some chocolate covered ... sigh) from another one of my families who chooses to pretend like she doesn't know that I get her game!

To top it all off, one sweet coworker treated me to lunch which was so fantastic—especially because I wasn't a fan of the random items I had haphazardly thrown into my lunch bag last night for today.

I'm generally not a fan of my birthday. In the past, I have usually chocked today up to the reality that it's becoming harder and harder to lie about my age. Replacing eyeliner for eyeglasses and eye cream. Trading nights out on the weekends for the sheer bliss of cuddling up in sweats that are too big but too inviting.

I want to thank everyone today who made me actually feel loved and special. I couldn't have imagined having such wonderful friends in my life a few years back. You will never know the profound effect your words and actions had on me today!

Thank you! Thank you!

Random Randomness, Part Four, 2013

Grant me the serenity to accept that it's time to purge my closet, the courage to part with items I always thought I might want to wear again, and the wisdom to know the difference between having a wardrobe and becoming a clothing hoarder. Amen.

***

Very sad that I'm watching *SpongeBob* with Lanie, and I'm secretly amused by the episode with the "bad word." Those of you who are brave enough to admit you've seen it will know what I'm talking about.

***

Nothing says Valentine's Day like waking up at 4 a.m., getting two kids off to daycare, working 8-5 with screaming little ones, racing home to get one to Girl Scouts until 7:30, racing home to get them ready for bed—and just as I am getting ready to force feed myself a garden burger for dinner, Sean becomes violently ill with the stomach flu. Arrrrrrrgh!

Cupid missed my bony ass when he shot his arrow this year. Screw flowers and romantic dinners. Bust out the ginger ale and Lysol.

***

Anyone else ever feel that, despite being blessed to have so much, there was a magic button to end feeling so anxious and lost? Just wondering if I'm alone in feeling this way?

***

So I'm preparing dinner tonight, and my beautiful seven-year-old walks in the kitchen full of innocent childhood wonder.

Dylanie: "Mommy, why does it hurt to have a baby?"

Me: "Hmmm, that's something we will talk about later together."

Dylanie: "But how do babies *get* in your belly?"

Me (deep breath): "Oh boy, baby, that's another thing you and I will talk about later."

Dylanie: "Okay, then can you tell me what 'explosive diarrhea' means?"

Folks, I couldn't make this 💩 up if I tried.

What happened to my baby girl in pull-ups with sippy cups? I'm going to bed. Wake me up when it's over.

***

I wish I were poolside with the smell of Coppertone on my skin and a scandalous book in my hand.

Woke up from an insane, disturbing dream where I worked as a super-max prison guard, and all they would give me for a method of defending myself was a tape measure and a flip phone to call for back up. I'm blaming a lost bet that I would try one of those homemade habañero-and-hot-sauce cookies last night.

***

Setting: 4:30 a.m., trying to make coffee with one eye barely open. The silence of the house is abruptly shattered with the shrill voice of a seven-year-old child who somehow managed to creep up behind me.

"Mommy! I peed my bed!"

Frustrated and on the verge of a heart attack from the shock of this unexpected intruder, I made my way into her room to strip her bedding, only to realize that she neglected to inform me that "peeing her bed" must have also meant she unloaded the equivalent of a water tank in her sleep.

It's gonna be one of those days … I just know it.

***

One thing about Logan is his inability to lie. When he woke up and said he felt 100% better, I asked if he felt good enough to go to school. Most kids would come up with every ailment to stay home. He just looked down and told me he supposed that would be a good idea.

***

Can't believe a day will ever come when my kids don't sit at my side on vacation with so much excitement. Makes me remember being little with my family at Hampton Beach and thinking how simple and magic vacation was. Time for lobster dinner and shopping for me finally. Hoodies and new belly button ring. Life is good, just for the moment. Sometimes I wish that I had a magic button that would forbid me from getting overwhelmed by them and learn to love these tiny moments in my chapter of life. They are truly my whole world.

***

Well, hello random summer rain. Thank you for the services. I was beginning to think I was sunbathing on the surface of hell

***

While sitting at the table this morning eating breakfast, Dylanie grabbed a stack of bills to be paid and said to Logan, "Wow, Mommy sure does get a lot of fan mail." Love, love, love that girl's thought process!

***

Did I miss the memo that it's National Drive Like a Geriatric Zombie Day? The roads are clear. Gas pedal is on the right people. You're welcome.

***

When I was looking at my daughter today as she was doing her own hair and had picked out a dress for her birthday, it struck me how lucky I was to watch her be such an independent little girl. I remember when I was twenty-one weeks pregnant, the doctors weren't optimistic that she would make it, never mind become the confident, outgoing person she's become. That proves the power in faith. It was worth every week in the hospital on bed rest, every blood draw and series of awful tests, and every prayer that we would make it "one more week" so that she wouldn't come into the world critically early.

It was all worth it.
The end.

***

Some things I've learned very recently the hard way—family is everything to me, and I should work to prove how much they mean in my life. And that I need to do everything in life that I put off because there isn't enough money, time, etc. Start crossing off the items on my bucket list and create new adventures and dreams to add to it. I'm learning that we have only today to strike, and each day after is but a gift we shouldn't feel is guaranteed.

***

Going fishing.
These times make me nostalgic about summers when I was little, pulling sunfish out of our lake on our dock with my grandfather there to teach me.
I miss being little.
When I was little, I didn't know that someday I would be 36 and miss being little.
Wonder if I will ever be 72 and miss being 36?
Could I ever find the same peace in the present that I found in my childhood memories?

***

Spent the majority of today cleaning my mortifying filthy house and came to a sad conclusion. I am *not* Martha Stewart, and while some complain about dust-bunnies in their homes, I have realized that my lack of Suzie Homemaker skills has forced me to accept that I have dust-yeties invading my home.
This is why I don't clean.
Ignorance is such bliss

***

Gratitude is when the biggest problem of my day was not finding cute boots while shopping that hug my skinny, chicken legs.

***

"Dylanie, did you brush your teeth?"
Points to mouth. "Duh, Mom. Do you want to take a whiff?"

***

There is nothing like having your eight-year-old daughter announce at sonic boom volume that "there are sure a lot of *elderlies* out today" in a crowded parking lot to make one want the ground to swallow them up.

***

Here are seven random facts about me:
1. I sleep with a blankie. I call it my "Nonie" and don't care about haters.
2. I don't like ice cream. I prefer the toppings.
3. I have never eaten steak in my life and can't even look at prime rib.
4. I actually like to eat Spam. Again, haters, don't judge.
5. I have never seen the *Matrix* movies, *Pulp Fiction*, or *Gone With the Wind*.
6. I have an irrational fear of worms … especially maggot-type crawlies.
7. I'm an adrenaline junkie and dream about sky diving someday.
Now you know.

***

—

A person with anxiety should know better than to attempt a trip to the new Walmart. The crowd here right now is making me begin to think there is something to the zombie apocalypse theory. Can't wait to be once again safe in my home again and finding peace in online shopping.

***

If anyone would like to brighten up my holidays, I would love whoever invented the fourth-grade musical recorder instrument to be brought bound and gagged to my home so that I can inflict insane harm. Possibly an eardrum injury would suffice. How much more can this girl take of the practicing of "Hot Cross Buns" before I need to be taken to the special doctor with the huggy vest and soft, padded room?

***

That awkward moment when you're trying to explain to your eight-year-old why her belting out lyrics from "Blurred Lines" is inappropriate. All I heard was, *"you know you want it."* Oy vey.

***

I was so thrilled that Logan read one of my childhood favorites, *Tales of a Fourth Grade Nothing,* and enjoyed it. When I told him what my favorite part of the book was, he replied, "Oh, so this is an *old* book!"
Really?
I'm grounding him just because.

***

It's official. My son got his first pimple. Albeit tiny, I dabbed Proactiv on it and told him it was a normal part of growing up.
Sounds benign enough, agreed?

67

I thought so too.

Until …

Dylanie pitched a minor fit and claimed I loved Logan more than her because he gets everything and she doesn't. And by "everything," she was referring to major orthodontic appliances and bad skin.

Guess I will have to prove my equal devotion to my daughter. After all, nothing says maternal love like sharing all the worst-case puberty effects with both children.

I wish, truly wish, I was exaggerating.

***

Against my better judgment, I decided to play "what does the fox say?" in the car for my children yesterday morning. I decided to break out my witty "cool" mom persona and sing the lyrics while dancing a fool to the obnoxious sound effects. Dylanie was delighted and sang along with me, enunciating the chorus lines in her attempt at car ride stardom.

Logan gazed out the window, seemingly bored and not actively phased by my giddy attempts at early morning entertainment. I figured he was pondering something deeper, something more educated than my performance.

I was correct.

When the song ended, his gaze broke from the outside view he was taking in, and he set me straight back into the reality of his literal thought processing ways of viewing the world.

He said, without missing a beat, "You do know Mom, a fox would never say those things."

Yes Logan, I'm aware.

***

Please help. My eight-year-old daughter is a toy/junk hoarder. The said child is currently away for the weekend. Please give me encouragement and the permission to raid her bedroom with industrial strength trash bags and throw away the carnage.

***

Driving in the car on our way to get pictures with Santa, Dylanie gazed out the window at the falling flurries. Warmth filled a deep part of my soul.

Oh yeah. You know what's coming

"I love this time of year. It's so cold that you don't have to play basketball outside without your shirt on."

***

I need a maid to clean this house and a sugar daddy to pay for her. Or I could just take a nap.

***

Last night I dreamed I was set up on a blind date with Raj from *Big Bang Theory*. He picked me up at my childhood house in a trolley from the Trolley Museum and told me he couldn't hold hands because of his "sweat gland problem." I too, was a hot mess sans bra. And he drove until his trolley opened up magically into a ritzy ballroom where we were to have an impromptu class of '95 reunion by the driving range on North Street in Enfield (near deck hockey). Then, he somehow produced my old class ring and told me he wanted me to wear it to "bring us to the next level."

Sooooo ...

I got up for the day at 3:50 a.m.

***

I loathe doing laundry … yet I'm not gonna lie. I still get excited when I find spare change at the bottom. Kinda like going to the casino for people with no life.

***

Figures I forgot to boil the eggs last night to make deviled eggs for Christmas Eve. It's obscenely early in the morning for my house to smell like a giant Sasquatch fart, but it's the price I have to pay for being a scatterbrain.

I wish I had a dog to blame it on.

***

I feel so violated. Only I could be at a Dunkin Donuts counter with a creepy dude standing *wayyyyy* too close behind me. I moved forward and he followed suit. Finally, I turned around asked him if I was in his way. Still plastered within my dance space, he replied, "No-no. I'm trying to figure out that amazing fragrance you're wearing."

Why me and why so damn often?

Creep magnet.

Devaluation

Years back, I worked for an intensive educational program for young individuals with profound autism and varying other special needs. As exhausting and overwhelming as it was at times, I revelled in being a critical aspect of providing my students with the skills they would need to develop simple qualities within their lives.

I studied and taught each student according to their individualized plans and spent many painstaking hours trying to extract the desired data and positive results that were demanded in black and white print on each plan.

But, most importantly, I greeted them every morning, reassured the angst-painted faces of their families at drop off, asked the students about their days and interests, cheered them on when they met a goal, gave them dignity when they needed an understanding human to help them tend to the personal care that they struggled with or couldn't tackle alone.

Upon my yearly evaluation, I received outstanding marks and was told that I was amazing at the knowledge I had in my chosen line of work.

And then came the "but."

But … I was marked at needing improvement in the area that involved me to keep 100 percent within the students' plans and to back off from, and I quote, "being so outwardly friendly with the kids. If you come in every day and make small talk with the students, they'll deviate from wanting to meet their goals because they'll think all they have to do is communicate with you about the niceties outside of the program."

Needless to say, I cried during my evaluation. I cried for myself, as I was being asked to be the kind of educator and human that I don't know how to be. I cried for my students, as I realized this world often looks at individuals with special needs as a set of trials on paper to check off in order to prove success and worth. In the eyes of my superior, I would only excel in my position if I began to look at my students—many families' beautiful miracle children—as a job rather than a person worthy of being treated as such.

I have no regrets in what I said at that evaluation. I won't air those words here, but I left with my head high and my heart aching.

We are all in this world together with our own, unique ways of breathing the same air, bleeding red, and trying to find the comforts in just being us.

Be kind. We never know what a smile or a soft word might do to brighten another's world.

Something Important

Logan wanted to surprise his sister by buying a DS game she wanted. He got ready to leave the house with Sean to head to Gamestop to buy it.

He had all of his allowance money in his hand.

All of it.

Me: "Logan, you are not using all of that cash to buy some ridiculous game."

Logan: "Yes I am. It's my money and I earned it. I'm using it to buy Dylanie what she wants for her birthday."

Me: "Why don't you get her something smaller and less expensive and save your money for something a little more important—maybe something important to you that you might want down the road!"

Logan: "I am. It's for my sister and she's important to me."

I've done something right. Something so incredibly right.

Or someone higher believed I needed to be blessed beyond anything money can buy.

Yes, little man, you are teaching me better than I have taught myself.

When I'm going through a rough patch in this crazy roller coaster called life, it's times like this that make me realize that I am so unbelievably blessed to have been given the opportunity to be a mother to such amazing miracles.

I've come to learn that, practicing being the kind and positive change that I want to see in the world has proven to make me a better and healthier person.

Times like this one in particular have shown me how being a strong role model for my children will make that change possible. Even in the smallest ways. I guess it opened my eyes to how much my children interpret the world through positive reinforcement and seeing the good in people.

Matter

I often wonder that, if given the opportunity to see internally what every individual around us is going through (or suffering through), would it help us become more patient, empathetic human beings?

Underneath every woman's perfectly applied makeup, under every designer outfit, under every seemingly confident smile and attitude, I believe there is a person who simply longs for someone to ask one simple question.

"Do you know how much you matter?"

We wake up, makeup, show up, smile, laugh, work hard, struggle, and often put on one hell of a show to prove that we are strong enough to endure our daily existences.

Yet, so many of us are fighting demons, tears, fears, doubts, and poisonous thoughts within our own psyches.

Kindness matters and love wins.

Sometimes we need to slow down and realize that others are in need of reassurance that they make up a major link in the chain of our daily successes.

You are all amazing. No matter the struggles within—realize how much you matter.

To My Dearest Kerri

The first time I watched *Frozen* was on a Wednesday morning while visiting my girl Kerri—a special day with an old friend.

That day was my introduction for this story of grace.

That particular visit was emotional. I had commented on the fact that I had always wished for the gift of being able to sing. Kerri shared her inner sadness for the fact that she knew she would never sing in the choir again. It was a moment that stands out in my mind. A lot.

This afternoon, my daughter and I were singing in the backyard. The songs? The *Frozen* soundtrack, of course!

Dylanie and I together as a melodic duo? Well, we truly are terrible.

Yet in the middle of the travesty of our singing, a butterfly landed on the grass in between us. It stayed throughout our backyard performance. It stayed long enough for me to remind Dylanie of the symbolic ways that Kerri shows us she's always "got our backs."

She loved me through all my faults and shortcomings. She loved everyone that way.

She stayed through our performance. I wonder if she fashioned, in her crafty ways, a set of butterfly earplugs.

Miss you sweet angel.

***

On the chance there's Wi-Fi in heaven, I wanted to let you know that I always try to keep my promises.

So long ago, I was envious of your cowboy boots as they were always something I dreamed of owning. I made you promise me that when you were up to it, you would join me in line-dancing lessons. We were gonna embrace our inner country girl and go Boot-Scootin' Boogying.

One day I promise to make you proud in some dive country bar-type environment with my newfound mad redneck skills.

However, my dear …

I need you to send me a sign Tuesday that I made you laugh from afar when I adorn my attire (at a beautiful gathering to celebrate that you were the angel who brought together, a village of people who became whole because of your amazing soul) with the cowboy boots I never got to wear with you at my side.

Don't worry. People will understand when they know of our plans.

And fear not, my friend, for I will not forsake you and attempt any moves on the dance floor as I will save those for the day we meet again.

See?

I try to keep my promises.

Love you always.

Always …

Me.

***

Out of the blue …

Logan: "Mom, I miss Kerri. I'm sad because I know she was your friend."

Me: "She was a friend to all of us."

Logan: "I just miss her. I'm sad because I saw you cry."

Me: "I cried because I love her. It's okay to cry when we hurt. I miss her like crazy."

Logan: "I wish we could text her some way. Do you wish that too?"

You have no idea my little man. Thank you for giving me a moment of your precious empathy.

***

"525,600 minutes, 525,000 moments so dear. 525,600 minutes. How do you measure, measure a year? Measure in love."

If not for the world my beautiful Kerri allowed me to become a part of, I would never have met the amazing friends I cherish so deeply.

I would never have learned to allow God into my heart and leaned on Him when the days seemed hopeless.

Conversations about how to handle the darkest days with faith and hope would never have taken place if I hadn't had the chance to pick up the phone and call Kerri in tears for guidance. (Even on her really difficult days, she was my protector and voice of strength.)

Never would her beautiful children have entered my children's life and brought fulfillment and laughter where loneliness had once been.

Never would I have been given the most precious of all gifts in learning how eternally strong the love of a mother and wife could be when faced with the ultimate decision: give in or fight fearlessly despite the pain and suffering that the battle would present.

Never would I have been taught how important it is to give of yourself what you can, without ever expecting anything in return. How good it feels to be the kind if person we were put in this Earth a short time to be.

I will love you eternally, Kerri. They say it takes a village to raise a child. You have a village who all can thankfully say they were blessed to have been a part of your beautiful world. This village and all its grateful members will never leave your family's side. We will continue to raise your beautiful angels with all the love and beauty you taught us to share.

I pray that you know this as you find peace and comfort after your long, amazing battle. I pray you take our love with you and can finally rest, knowing we will never forget that we all became a part of your life for a reason. Maybe when I'm angry by everything you had to endure, I can feel peace by that reason.

And when I get to see you again someday, you owe me a night of line dancing and Twinkies.

Never goodbye … just see you again.

***

My entire life, I had avoided the idea of being close to a loved one as the journey on the earth grew close to the end. I suppose this was due to my own fears about coming to terms with feeling anguish, pain, fear, and emptiness.

Last year on this day, I lost a friend who came into my life for a reason. She taught me that death was not to be feared as much as life was meant to be cherished. She taught me about stopping to enjoy the things I complain about every day, as they are gifts from God that are put into my life as lessons.

To adore my children when they are being unlovable, for they are of my own blood and soul.

To laugh at myself when I am flawed because we are only able-bodied for the moment.

To cry when I'm sad, for the toughest times make the happy times more worthwhile.

I'm glad that I made the decision to visit Kerri as she was nearing the end of her life and tell her how much I would never lose sight of what she taught me about living my own life. I'm glad I got to lay in her arms and cry with her without fear of what was to come.

But most of all, I'm just thankful that Kerri *was*. To know that Kerri will always *be* as she lives on in the hearts of those who were lucky enough to have known her.

***

After a recent soccer game, Dylanie stopped as she was walking off the field to gently scoop a butterfly from the grass.

As it rested on the tip of her finger, she said to all of us, "Look! It's Kerri!"

And just like that, we felt a sense of beautiful peace that cannot be fully expressed with words.

Miracles are always waiting for us in the smallest, most unusual places and times.

I Would've

If I had my life to live over, I would've learned to tell others how much I loved them a lot more often.

I would've been brave enough to have learned to say "I love you" years before it felt too late to make a difference.

I would've learned that friends come and go, but family is forever.

I would've learned that it was okay to not be okay.

I would've learned to fall in love with the smell of my newborn's head instead of wishing away the sleepless nights.

I would've laughed more at the antics of the toddler years, instead of worrying about my messy home.

I would've cried when I needed someone to listen, instead of feeling weak and embarrassed that I was human.

I would've been brave enough to say I had tattoos and crazy memories years before I had the guts not to hide them.

I would've not felt awkward when simply saying, "I love you" to my loved ones because it felt awkward in my own, difficult fashion.

I would've accepted hugs, even if my boundaries didn't want to allow.

I would've been there more. When shit was scary. When I didn't know how to be there "the right way."

But I didn't. I can't reverse time.

I have my life to live now. Not the life I ever envisioned. I still shy away from hugs and the sappy shit. I have tattoos and a past that makes me laugh and shudder. I have learned the art of crying when I'm hurt, of the intoxicating smell of a sleeping child's hair and how the words "I love you" aren't so scary.

Not one of us will ever be perfect. However, if we live as though tomorrow won't be a gift, we might make baby steps so as to not have to write about what we may have done if we had doubts.

Peace and love always.

We Trusted

A man we know has just been charged with the murder of his wife. So many of us trusted this man as we cared for his children. We were there to help him and Connie find answers for their sweet little boy's medical issues.

So many of us loved this family. We believed that we saw what a loving marriage was made of.

So many of us loved Connie. Her love for her family was something made from the strongest passion to fight for her child. She gave her all to make sure that her son had every opportunity to get the care he needed.

So many of us saw her smile all the time, when it was obvious that she forced it so that others never saw her pain.

She will always be our beautiful friend. Memories don't lie.

She was a beautiful person for us to keep safe in our memories.

We trusted this man.

He took our friend away. He took away a beautiful mother to two amazing little boys. He took away his "role" as their father.

I feel so jaded. I'm broken inside. I don't understand how we didn't see it. I always see the silver linings.

I feel so devastated.

I'm glad he didn't make bond. How dare he make a statement claiming innocence?

I hope he never sees the outside of a prison community again.

I pray that Connie's boys find peace and always remember the love that she bestowed upon them.

We trusted this man. So long ago.

You All Matter

To everyone in my life who feels like they are failing somehow:

You are a wonderful mom/dad/grandparent, etc. Don't think that because you aren't "Pinterest perfect" that your children don't adore you. PB&J will fill their bellies just as much as a lunch that looks like something Donna Reed would bow down to. At the end of the day, will they remember the perfectionist meal put into their lunch box or the nighttime snuggles and hugs?

You are doing your best at your job. We are human. We make mistakes and we grow from them. Go the extra mile whenever you can, even if you just do it for yourself. Give yourselves a pat on the back. Be grateful to have a job and elated to have one that you love.

You are beautiful. Unless you have someone to airbrush what you feel looks like Hollywood perfection and the ability to photoshop what you think isn't acceptable in a fantasy world. Love yourself. Love what's inside and love (or lovingly accept) what makes up your outer canvas. Who you are externally does not make up who you are and what you give to the world.

And don't sweat the pimples, wrinkles, freckles, small lips, big lips, eyebrows, nose, etc. Embrace your unique self. Someday, you will wish you had back what you have today. Someday, you will want back the very thing that looks back at you in the mirror at this stage in your life.

You can't be everything. Give yourself a break. There will always be people who don't care for you, and that's okay. There will always be bills to pay and errands to run and appointments to make. There will always be disappointments and not enough time. There will always be things left on your to-do list that are not crossed off. There will always be days where you feel stretched to your limit and not as worthwhile as you really are.

Let it go.

Easier said than done, I understand. But each and every one of us needs the opportunity to realize that we are in this life together.

This is not a dress rehearsal. Put your best foot forward and understand that you are everything you need to be to somebody in this world. Your best and your all are the only things you can give.

That's what makes each one of you in my life amazing.

You all matter. You all make a difference.

You are doing just fine.

Spectrum

I was told once that, in the age of a social media boom, talking about my son having autism might label him for life.

I took this concept into consideration for a while. I went through the "what ifs" immensely about whether or not being honest about his diagnosis with others would be a setback for him down the road.

And then, last year, we had the big talk with him. Not the talk about how babies are made or the magical idea of Santa being in our hearts—but the open, raw discussion about how his mind worked in different and beautiful ways. We discussed how everyday things might come with difficult to him at times, while perplexing concepts for most "neurotypicals" might, for him, be second nature. We discussed his fears and his quirks. We answered his questions. We read books on autism spectrum disorders. We sat at times in silent reflection.

And I knew right away that being open to the world and to my son about his unique, confusing, sometimes frustrating, always breathtaking ways of understanding his world was the right decision. I knew because he owned it like a badge of honor.

A light went on in his immediate cognition that made it so apparent to all of us there that he finally had an answer. An answer for just him that made, what I am sure, millions of anguishing moments become clear and finally acceptable to him.

In a nutshell, letting him in on the unique (albeit concise) reasoning as to why he is the amazing child he is gave him insight to move forward.

He doesn't shy away either. Don't be shocked someday if you bump into my little buddy and get an earful about protons, atmospheric pressure, *any* video game character, girls (ugh), and Asperger's.

I am one hell of a lucky woman to have been so blessed with a little boy who is raising me up as I raise him.

Winner

I wanted to share a truly heartwarming moment that literally almost moved a bunch of us to tears this afternoon.

Today at our mother/daughter tea with Girl Scouts, Dylanie and I bought a ton of raffle tickets and tried our luck at winning some of the really cool prizes up for offer. Winning number after winning number was called and, unfortunately, this year we weren't as lucky as in the past. Dylanie was clearly disappointed, but was really mature about being a good sport as her friends won various prizes.

Out of the blue, a friend's daughter walked over to Dylanie and handed her the necklace she had won—the necklace Lanie really loved and had tried to win. She told Dylanie that, because she had already won another prize, she wanted to make sure that Lanie had something to go home with also.

That selfless act, along with the genuine way in which she did it, was such an amazing moment and proof that she is being raised to be a wonderful young lady. I was truly touched that someone that young showed proof that the world *is* a better place when we practice random acts of kindness.

Something you May not Know

If anyone feels that this post warrants a response that is rude or offensive instead of insightful, kindly keep on scrolling.

Regardless of anyone's personal feelings about Connecticut Governor Malloy and his decisions, people need to step back before they make cruel, nasty remarks about the manner in which he speaks.

Many may not realize that he has battled a speech disorder (somewhat similar to Tourette syndrome) throughout his life and still struggles when speaking. I'm pretty sure it's something he is constantly aware of and is probably insecure about. As with any person with a special need or physical/intellectual impairment, bullying and lack of compassion is wrong and ignorant.

Whether or not you are a fan of Malloy or the way he makes his decisions as our governor, that is strictly your business. However, please keep in mind that making public references about another person's personal deficits is cruel and shows that there is a definite need for more acceptance of those with special needs of any kind.

Whether a high-ranking official or a stranger passing by on the street, we are all human beings sharing/surviving this world together. If we all worked harder to love one another for our beautiful, unique differences and kept the intolerance and hatred at bay, we would soon discover that all of our imperfections are only a fraction of what makes us amazing and capable.

Choose love!

Love is a Bonfire

Many of you who know me well know that I am a chronic germophobe. However, if you *really* know me well, you know that I do have a huge heart and tend to carry the burden of worry about others.

So. With that being said, I have figured out a way to mend every broken branch this evening.

Sean is really sick with the stomach flu. I, like everyone, can find empathy in what he is dealing with.

And I *always* find a way and a silver lining when faced with dilemma.

I checked to make sure he was comfortable and that he had his favorite blanket.

I then feverishly stripped every god-forsaken fabric off our bed and considered burning them, only to realize I was being overly dramatic. They are sitting in scorching hot water in the washer where I will wash them over and over again until they are thread bare and rid of evil vomit ions. After that, I may use them to clean the bathroom before disposing of them. That, however, might cause a cling-on puke/shit germ to attach itself to my favorite seat in the house.

I feel a trip to Bed Bath and Beyond coming in the near future.

But I did lovingly strip the bedding. That way, when I do actually allow his ass back into the bedroom, there will be brand new bedding to sleep on.

By the way, anyone interested in a ginormous bonfire when I decide to burn the couches?

Socks

Without hearing about "how I should tell them the truth," I'm feeling like a time of motherhood mourning is creeping up upon the impending end to the magic of Christmas morning with my babies. A classmate of Logan told him that Santa wasn't real. Yes, I know he is ten, and it was an inevitable issue I was doomed to tackle at one point … but …

I have but precious few components left in my "get out of jail free" white-lie exceptions when it comes to accepting that my babies are falling into that category where they are straddling the fence into big kid reality.

I guess I'm not ready to let go.

I need one more year of that magical Christmas morning—a morning of pajama-clad, exhilarated Muller child "Santa came!" expressions on the faces of the children that I had begrudgingly (to put it PG-rated) spent months doing all I can to make their holiday dreams come true.

I teach my children never to lie. However, I'm willing to put my dignity aside to scrape up whatever I can to sacrifice one last year of faith and the belief in the magic of St. Nick from my children.

The reality of how fast our children grow up is a tad heart wrenching.

I hope the child that tried to prematurely steal the one last season of magic from my little boy asked for an Xbox for Christmas.

And gets socks.

Traditions

I do my deepest life pondering and random thinking on my daily commutes to work. Today's cranium party had me thinking about family traditions and how I had once had visions of my family gathered around the breakfast table. I envisioned me, make-up perfect, smiling at my precious children while serving homemade, organic waffles, steaming from a pat of melted butter and maternal love.

Cue the reality of the breakfast table (aka, junk-mail collector, random, forgotten Happy Meal toy wrapper vortex, fossilized crumb museum) and the insanity that ensues with trying to keep my children alive with whatever keeps the meltdowns to a minimum. Now delete that image of any resemblance to a human female when you picture the '50s prototype I had once dreamed of becoming.

Made from scratch waffles be damned. I don't care that the Pop Tart tastes stale. We don't have time to nuke it. Eat it and be thankful. There are children in this world who don't have stale Pop Tarts!

And then there's the insatiable need to out-do the other sibling with the loudest, most ground-moving flatulence contest. At the breakfast table! Both children are contestants, and my precious angel girl usually takes first prize with Logan getting the participation ribbon and giggles as a consolation prize.

Traditions, I have come to learn, are not traditional.

Enough Difference

Sometimes it takes me digging through my bag after a long day and pulling out a colored-pencil drawing that was handed to me with an angelic voice proclaiming, "I made this for you Miss Trisha," that makes the world okay in my eyes.

Makes the exasperated, slightly inappropriate utterances to my child, after forgetting her soccer bag on the way to practice, so meager in comparison to real life issues. It means I have a healthy child who plays sports and made human mistakes.

Makes the fact that my dishwasher died an inconvenient death a reminder that I have a home and food to dirty the dishes.

Makes the fact that I didn't have the chance to eat my lunch a reminder that I was too swept up in guiding my sweet friends in class to realize my tummy was talking.

Makes me realize that I *do* have the ability to slow the hell down and appreciate life on my terms. That I am not dictated by work, sports, chores, homework, meetings, grocery shopping, scout badges, and what is deemed "the dream" by those who honestly don't matter in the realm of life.

I make enough difference in the life of a child to receive a piece of art that was drawn on her own time.

I make enough difference.

Thank you to my sweet friend for putting a smile on my face this evening. Your tiny act turned my day around to what is so crucial in this world.

Random Randomness, Part Five, 2014

Dear guilty person who made our shared bathroom at work "less than pleasant."

While I appreciate you thinking of your fellow colleagues by masking the "issue" you created with dollar store Magnolia and Cherry Blossom room spray, I *do* have one simple, eensy-weensy request.

Based on the fact that I nearly needed a military-grade gas mask to find my way through the florally fog, can you possibly not be so over-eager next time number two comes a-callin'?

Your cooperation in this matter is greatly appreciated.

Sincerely,

Trisha—a girl who only needed to pee, not become sterile/radioactive.

***

Sometimes, weird as it sounds, the smell of my children's hair puts me where I need to be.

When I hug them, of course. I don't chase my kids around sniffing their hair. Just clarifying.

***

My house is a mess.
The dishes are piled high.
Bills are stacked on the desk.
My house is warm.
My babies are tucked in and safe.
Tonight I am okay with this.

***

Getting my kids up and ready on school mornings can be likened to squeezing a greased pig into spandex. That's all.

***

Dylanie wanted to play Barbies with me tonight and after stripping them down to what God blessed them with, she covered them up and said, "Don't look at her bad parts."

I explained that she didn't need to cover them up, as we females all have the same parts.

Her response?

"We don't have the same taste buds, or earwax, or boogers. Sooooo, you're not correct."

Touché little girl. Touché.

***

You know what? I've learned so much this past week.

I've learned that, although I have the inner need to find hatred in people and situations, I simply won't. Nor will I seek revenge out of anger. That simply can't be me.

No, I have learned something far greater.

I have love and the ability to love. I have the ability to fight and to attempt to see through the tears to a brighter tomorrow.

And I have friends and family.

I have it all.

It took going through hell to understand that I have more blessings in my life than I realized.

So bring it, world.

I have an army of amazing people to pick me right back up.

***

Me to Dylanie: "How was school today?"

Dylanie with the everyday answer: "Good."

Me: "Well, did you learn anything new or exciting?"

Dylanie: "Yup. I sure did."

Long pause ensues.

Me: "Are you going to tell me what you learned about today?"

And as many of you already know, sometimes I just don't want to know what answer I'm about to walk into.

Dylanie: "I learned today that the janitor at my school chopped off his pinky when he was thirteen."

I could go on, but I bet you get the point.

***

My children are playing baseball in the backyard. In the muddy, pre-spring-clean-up backyard.

My kids are going to come in the house dirty and sweaty. Covered in kid grime.

I am one happy mom for that.

***

So, after finding out that Dylanie forgot her book fair money today, you know I just *had* to swing by her school with my checkbook because (A) I'm a huge advocate of early literacy, and (B) because every parent knows the travesty in being eight years old without book fair money).

There's nothing like showing up unannounced at your child's school to make you feel like a celebrity. As Lanie introduced me to everyone (I'm surprised the janitor got away unscathed), I was all ready to break out a Bic and sign autographs.

These are the moments I won't forget. I know the time is approaching when showing up at my children's school will be devastatingly mortifying rather than full of Hollywood stardom.

When that time comes, I will show up in my bathrobe and slippers.

***

I love my schoolkids and I love education. But it's hard to be around my kids when school lunch was Mexican food.

***

While I'm tucking Logan into bed tonight, he asks me why girls sometimes have hair on their legs but grown women don't.

I was perfectly honest with him in explaining that "Women shave their legs as they get older. Us women do strange things that boys don't have to do."

His reply?

"Forget it. I don't want to hear any more."

But Logan! I was just getting to the good stuff!

***

Just heard an odd ruckus outside followed by my children conversing with on another in strange prose and tone.

I had to investigate, so I opened the door and gave them my infamous inquiring look.

Only to be answered—no commanded—by my daughter to go back inside as they were "pretending to be old people."

Well hell, it sure beats the Xbox, even it it's disturbing and quite frankly creepy.

But whatever keeps them from killing each other is fine by me.

***

Shame on me. Seriously.

My daughter asked me to play Apples to Apples with her and Logan, and I had the nerve to say I was too tired from a long day.

A day that involved me teaching young children. Children who weren't my own.

Needless to say, *I'm playing the damn game.*

These are those times you can't get back.

Forget regret or life is yours to miss.

***

I decided to give Lanie a spa pedicure with all the luxuries: foot bath, lotion, polish—the works.

It was going to be a picture-perfect mother/daughter moment between my little girl and me.

Let's just say that my moment of sentiment ended abruptly when I looked close at her bony, eight-year-old legs and realized they were silky smooth.

Yeah. That just happened. And she actually tried to lie and say she did it by accident.

Sadly enough, she shaved her legs better than I shave my own.

But still. This isn't okay.

***

On the water today, a tiny boat passed by me.

A three-seater aluminum boat with a tiny Evinrude motor putted by.

And the smell of two-stroke from the little boat motor brought me back to a place in my life when I can honestly say I remember peace.

I was back in time, with my grandfather at my side. My grandfather, teaching a little girl about the ins and outs of a simple boat motor. Gas, choke, 1, 2, 3 …

A little girl, her grandfather, an antique reel, and a can of night crawlers. A pull on the line, bobber underwater. To a little girl, it was the Walter of all fish … and we always let him go.

Poor maimed pumpkinseed. To me, you were my summer memories.

A time I will cherish and never get back.

But … that smell of two-stroke. Like a dream you awaken from and cannot explain to another for fear of them not understanding its worth.

A memory that is my own to cherish.

I miss the times that have now become nothing more than memories I can only visit in the passing of a stranger's tiny vessel.

***

Just told my son, "Don't worry, buddy. Eventually we'll find friends for you to hang out with in the neighborhood."

I watched him ride away down the driveway alone. It awakened such a sadness and longing inside of me.

He has his little sister and he has us to keep his mind entertained.

He should have so much more.

Holy crap moment: I just slapped myself figuratively as I wrote those last words.

In the scheme of real life, especially lately, I should be ashamed.

Not of my feelings, as they are real and okay. I tell my children this often.

But that I just downplayed my role in his world.

Gonna put this phone down for a few. My son is calling for a game of mom-and-son paddleball.

***

Dear crotchety neighbor,

In my opinion, summer is finally here.

In my opinion, summer around here involves high-energy children, laughs around a warm, summer evening fire, and fireworks.

Yep, fireworks.

You're more than welcome to join our celebration on the Fourth of July. Perhaps an extra dose of Geritol and an extra nap that day will bring a smile to that rickety attitude.

Refreshments will be served. Feel free to bring an appetizer.

Best regards,

Your neighbor two houses up.

P.S. When planning an appetizer, please keep in mind that I don't eat meat but do enjoy something Cajun and zesty.

***

Logan: "Dylanie, when you're a grown-up and move away, will you live close to me?"

Dylanie: "Yeah, why?"

Logan: "So I know you're close in case I need you to help me."

Thank you, God, for those beautiful miracles.

***

Dylanie: "Mom, isn't 'psychotic' such a cool word? It's like, so much fun to say."

***

Oh, my anxiety riddled brain …

I've waited and worked so hard all year to take my children on vacation.

Why do you have to make packing such a frightening process? Why do you force me to feel like my children might develop some aggressive third-world virus and that I should pack circumstantial meds?

Or that a blizzard might sweep over the beach so I should pack arctic apparel?

Can't you just let me relax and enjoy my vacation while giving a well-deserved imaginary middle finger to this past year?

I will obsess double-duty when we get home if you grant said request.

Please and thank you.

***

This time tomorrow, my family and I should be arriving at our vacation paradise in Old Orchard Beach.

We saved our change all year to be able to make our yearly trip a reality.

What a year it's been. One that certainly had more if its shares of downward spirals than upward.

Can't wait to smell the salt air and walk barefoot on the sandy beach. Can't wait to hear my children's laughter as they venture into waves *far* too cold for me to join in.

Can't wait to clear my head of all that has hurt my heart this year and breathe in all that is to be.

And did I mention my children's laughter?

***

My son makes me laugh, in all of his sweet perseverations.

This afternoon he happened to get wind that his sister wanted to write her own stage play, to be brought to life in my backyard.

And he just can't let it go.

"I need to learn everything about this play so I can write a book based on it."

All stinking afternoon he honestly wanted me to eavesdrop on her and her little friend planning their new Broadway phenomenon.

So he could steal the rights to her storyline and write a book.

He's ten. He's so damn cute.

Proud and tired mommy!

***

Dylanie token comment of the day: "Ah man, this bathing suit is starting to give me a butt crack."

Sometimes I figure it's best to let sleeping dogs lie—and to let creeping fabric creep.

***

Logan: "When is lunch? I usually have lunch between 11-12. I just want to know."

Me at the waters edge: "Just relax and enjoy the beach. We'll have lunch in like a hour or so."

Logan: "Okay, but after we eat it's time we skedaddle up to the pool."

Apparently, my son is ten going on eighty.

Skedaddle!?

***

Why oh why is my eight-year-old talking about liking a boy in her class?

Why, oh, why did she not only use the term "make out," but also utter those words in my presence?

—

Does she *not* understand that I am capable of becoming her worst nightmare if she dares to become boy crazy at an early age?

Disclaimer: The term "worst nightmare" refers to, and is not limited to, quitting my job and sitting with her in class, lunch, and extracurricular activities throughout her school years wearing a house dress without a bra, curlers in my hair, face cream lopped on three inches thick, fluffy socks with orthopedic shoes, my night guard, breathe-right strips, and the New Testament opened and preached.

Don't mess little girl. I've got only my kids, a sick imagination, and a lot of time to put my thoughts into motion.

***

My son loves to chase and frighten the seagulls on the beach.

In other news, our blanket area is always barren because of pissed off French Canadian families who dislike getting crapped on by frightened seagulls.

I don't speak French, but I'm assuming I will know some four-letter words in French by the end of the week.

***

My son is the kindest soul.

First, he sees a little boy at the arcade walking around looking sad, and he offers him his quarters so he can play skeeball.

Then, when he is done cashing in his tickets (which he spent the rest of a year's worth of allowance money on, he tells his sister, without a second thought, "Here Dylanie. I will split my tickets with you so you get a bigger prize."

I did something right somewhere along the way. I'm so proud of them.

***

Last day of vacation, and I'm trying to hide from that sinking feeling of impending reality tomorrow.

Sunny and 75 degrees.

I could choose to cry because it's ending, or I can choose to find so much gratitude because it happened.

Either way, I know we made some sacred memories.

Thank you, God, for giving me this week to learn my children a little more. To know that, as exhausting as it was, I was given the gift of one week to thoroughly enjoy watching my two miracles bicker, laugh, play, and be young at the ocean.

If I never have tomorrow, I'm grateful that I have learned never to take a day with them for granted.

I love my perfect world of quirky imperfections.

***

This morning, I came to a trifecta of profanity-inducing reasons why I am a self-proclaimed terrible housekeeper.

In very particular order:

1. I don't *do* spring cleaning. I do "I can't figure out whether to seed the garden or the hardwood floors" cleaning.

2. My family must interpret "pick up after yourself" as "toss as much random shit all over the house and don't forget to step on each cereal flake you sprinkle like wretched fairy dust until it's a powdered, crack-like, ant-beckoning agent."

3. I made the mistake of moving my couches to vacuum under.

In case anyone's interested, I'm pretty sure I found Amelia Earheart and Jimmy Hoffa living together in enough cat hair to produce a yeti.

***

Dylanie quote of the week: "Mom, from now on please buy only the *tomato* kind of ketchup. This is delicious!"

***

On my immediate to-do list:

1. Start being more positive about life. Apparently, I have been giving off the impression that I'm frantic and unhappy. Anxiety is a hard issue to mask with a smile. I need to squelch my worries deep inside and find more gratitude in what is good and celebratory within my life. Contrary to how I come off to some, I don't need to be saved. Yet.

2. I need to give into the little moments that will someday be a distant memory. Like my little girl painting my nails hooker red and acting as though she had transformed me into a super model.

I'm glad that she is super intelligent and loves to learn. I pray that she uses her energy someday to become a veterinarian or scientist. She's a little rusty in the nail-tech department.

3. And I want—no, I need—to work on my resting-bitch-face syndrome. For the love of God, I need to smile more so I stop giving off the impression that I massacre small woodland animals for fun.

Just sayin'.

***

For the love of the Mommy Gods, please remove the phrase "but there's nothing to *do*" from my children's vocabulary.

If it doesn't involve electronics, they act as though I am asking them to perform electroshock therapy on themselves ... outside ... in the rain ... while walking on thumbtacks ... barefoot.

I curse the day I introduced the evil villain Minecraft into their worlds. I simply thought it was a great rainy-day game that they could play together while using their imaginations.

That's what I thought. In reality, it became all consuming. I set a timer for them to play and get the bends when it goes off as they react like the apocalypse is starting (the apocalypse that is masked in the form of me shooing their behinds outside to play).

Makes me wonder how on earth this generation would have ever survived my childhood. The abuse we suffered in spending our summer, you know, playing outside.

Holy crap. The blasphemy of life we were a part of back then.

***

It's days like today, kayaking with my daughter through the swampy waters in search of turtles and bullfrogs, that make me proud that my daddy raised me to be a little redneck country girl!

And I'm proud to say I'm raising my little girl to never be afraid to get a little dirty.

***

I wonder what it feels like to be my female friends on Facebook who always post about having such a blissful, pampered, happy life.

That isn't a mean shot either.

Please, tell me. Is it that amazing or is everyone's life photoshopped to share only the pretty aspects?

***

I've come to the realization that I'm the kinda girl who would love to have a country love song written for her, to be shamelessly adored through symbolic country melody.

And no, not a song about my dog dying or a leaky trailer. Or men who fish or get into bar brawls either.

Just a song to make me have the warm girly fuzzies is all I ask.

***

Yesterday I yearned for my comfy bed all day. Last night, I couldn't wait to rest my weary body amongst my pillows and sprawl out with bliss.

And I did.

I got so satisfyingly comfortable wrapped in my comforter as I awaited the gift of slumber to fall over me.

Only to realize, as I tucked my blankets in just the right configuration around my body, that my cat had pissed all over my duvet—the duvet that covers my comforter.

The comforter that I was in a near intimate embrace with as I was cocooned in its newfound use as a feline latrine.

Apparently, kitty had gotten locked all day in my room and couldn't cross his legs any longer. My bed served as a cozy loo for the furry bastard.

Yeah. Go on ahead and laugh at my demise.

***

I suppose I should actually get off the couch to clean my house. It works better that way.

We clean so thoroughly at work that I'm motivated to start doing it at home, but it's Saturday and I'm a schlump.

It's just so overwhelming. I never know where to start.

I know people see my kitchen first. That should be a starting point.

Should be.

But my bathroom and living room are screaming at me for a facial.

Don't get me started on the cat hair and kid crumbs so prominent on my hardwood floors that you could: A. Make a new cat, and B. Plant seeds in the crumb carnage and reap an entire crop of cereal plants.

Okay, that was a little extreme.

But. *Help!*

***

Perhaps my daughter doesn't believe me when I say I will toss the items she leaves all over the *Hoarders* episode of a bedroom she owns.

I mean, really. Am I speaking another language? Does "make sure your bedroom is picked up" translate into "dump random crap evenly throughout the sleeping quarters so that it takes Matrix moves to navigate your room"?

Should I take the plunge while she's away and make magic?

Is it bad that I feel powerful and riddled with guilt if I blow through her room like a lunatic with a forklift?

This isn't an open question. It warrants your support.

***

Lately I've been making it a priority to smile whenever possible and give of myself to others in ways to brighten their days. Even though the gestures are small, I love to know that I've brought some sort of positive experience to another human.

It's really changed my mood. It feels so good to choose happiness and pay it forward.

And it's way cheaper than therapy!

***

C'mon, Ambien … do your thing.

Sleep would be fantastic.

And by sleep, I do not mean endless nightmares about my teeth falling out, coupled with waking up every half hour to be reminded what time it is.

It's a small request. I don't ask for much.

***

I don't care how old my little boy is. At eleven, he asks me every night to sit next to him in his bed and rub his back for exactly one minute.

And each time he still tells me that he loves me.

These are the times we never get back.

***

Dylanie: "Mom, can I give you a makeover?"

Me: "No and it's time for bed."

Dylanie: "Awww, but there's nothin' to do and the cat won't let me give her one."

Swear to God that was word for word.

***

Feeling so anxious.

My kids start school tomorrow. I'm not ready. Every single year, I'm never ready.

How can it be that they aren't in pull-ups, Carter's clothes, walking around with sippy cups anymore?

Am I being punked? Where is the pause and enjoy button???

***

Breakthrough moment! Albeit a little sick and twisted.

My kids had been at each other's throats since we got home. We had forty-five minutes until soccer practice to eat and get ready. I was at a breaking point. Threatening and disciplining were proving beyond ineffective.

I brought out the big guns.

"Fine, you win! If you two are gonna argue instead of being loving to one another, I'm going to cry! That's it's! You win! Your behavior had made your mom cry!"

Silence. Terrified faces.

More silence.

Yep. That's more like it.

***

How is it possible that I went an *entire* day wearing bright orange underwear with stars all over them *and* leggings that were *completely transparent* and *nobody* told me!?

***

I just got my ass handed to me in a way that taught me a lesson.

Logan asked me a question about something pertaining to my everyday tasks. I responded to him by telling him that I didn't "have a life."

He came back at me with, "Yes you do. You have me."

I. Was …

I.

Was.

Speechless and remorseful.

***

Giving myself a pat on the back.

My son is so little that he literally needed a belt to keep his jeans up. On my lunch break today, I went to Burlington Coat Factory to look for a belt for him.

My son is now the proud owner of a new belt and this mommy left the store without buying new shoes for herself.

I know, right!?

***

My daughter is so extroverted that I get frightened to bring her in public. Meanwhile, my son keeps introducing himself to my coworkers by saying, "Hi, I have autism."

***

It just hit me this morning like a door slammed from my whining nine-year old.

Bam!

The realization that I have become that unshowered, Pop Tart serving, bathrobe-wearing at inappropriate times, threatening to runaway from bickering kids to another country, eating the Happy Meal scraps from my children for dinner, Facebook-addicted, Girl Scout and soccer mom that I had promised myself would never happen. I forgot to add that my list includes, but is not limited to, special-needs mom whose Aspie son has decided to take up the *trumpet* in order to solidify the increase in mom's medication intake.

I make that "old person" grunting sound when I get up off the couch, and my idea of paradise is taking my bra off and washing my makeup off to watch reality shows on a Friday night.

Somewhere in this universe is a barren castle with royal servants who are scratching their heads wondering where their queen is.

I'd Google directions to my palace, but I have to beat this impossible level in Candy Crush first.

And shower.

***

Today was one of those days where I should have followed my gut instincts and stayed in bed with the covers pulled up over my head so I could've cried out loud in the privacy of my own comfort.

Tomorrow simply has to be a day where I don't question the hows, whys, and whats of this journey called parenthood.

***

I just joined some amazing Girl Scouts delivering cookies to our local veterans to say thank you for all they sacrificed for our freedom. Our experience was very fulfilling and very emotional.

It's hard to believe that so many veterans were so surprised that this small, kind gesture came their way. I came away understanding that it's so important to teach our children never to forget those who sacrificed.

***

I miss the years when Christmas shopping for my children meant they ended up having more enjoyment playing with the boxes their toys came in instead of asking for random crap that may very well result in the remortgaging of my house.

***

Today, if Asperger's had a face, I would knock it on its ass.

If an assignment asks for a child to describe five reasons why they like the color orange and said child doesn't care for the color orange, guess what? You can explain all you want how they can "just be imaginative" and "make up" their reasons.

The joke's on you.

People with Asperger's don't play the white-lie game. That's just how it is.

Someday, I will revel a lot more in the fact that he can't lie.

Tonight, I want to cry.

And drop an "F-bomb"

A lot.

***

And to add to the fun that is this week, the kids on my daughter's bus told her that Santa isn't real—and that parents lie and leave their presents under the tree.

If I didn't love children so much, I'd be *that* mom on the five-o'clock news that went ape-shit on a school bus filled with children stealing the last glimmer of magic in my child's holiday.

But I love children that much.

I'm not going down just yet.

***

I look like such a bat-shit mess that I'm driving out of my way to grocery shop where I am less likely to frighten people I know.

***

Last night, Lanie was crying and Logan came up to me to ask me why. I explained that she was just having a tough night and was upset. He looked so forlorn and said, "I feel so bad for my sister."

My heart warmed with pride for his expression of empathy.

He then proceeded to walk over to her to wrap his arms around her and plant a kiss on her head. I was so close to brewing over with tears, when Dylanie jumped away as though she had been burned with a fire poker and began feverishly wiping off the top of her head.

The icing on the cake came when she screamed, "that's *disgusting!* Don't you *ever* do that to me again!"

Well, it *was* nice for a moment.

***

I know a lot of you are gonna be jealous at my most recent boast as a mother, but I'm willing to overlook the haters with envy for my world.

Only I could have a daughter who, in the span of one month, would question the validity of Santa and the cold, hard facts about menstruation.

Can you guess which topic she pushed until I had to break and squirm while I divulged the terms and details to my precious angel?

Hint: she still believes she has to be good for goodness sake.

Yes folks, 'tis the season for St. Nick and Kotex conversations.

***

So our "Elf on a Shelf" (named Shirley) has been a huge, fun success!

So successful that Lanie informed me that we should get a boy elf for Shirley. You know, so "they can make baby elves."

Tidings of Yuletide cheer, I think not!

***

So the kids and their dad put their tree up tonight.

Bring on the warm feelings of the holiday spirit.

And then the tree tipped and fell over.

Joe: "Stupid whore!" (To the tree of course.)

Joe uprights the tree so that decorating can ensue.

Logan comes back downstairs: "Dad, you fixed the whore?"

The funny part is, I think Logan might have actually believed that "whore" was a different term for the tree.

***

Sean and I are doing our yearly ritual of watching *Home Alone* and finding ridicule in the fact that *every* injury sustained by the two burglars would've most definitely resulted in paralysis or death.

Don't ask. It's just what we've always done.

***

Hiding and sobbing in the bedroom while Lanie watches the end of *Marley and Me*.

Nope.

Can't do it.

***

Sean just saw me curled up in a ball on the couch.
He brought me a pillow and asked me if I wanted chocolate.
I will skip the throat punch and keep him!

***

I'm not making a resolution for the new year.

Instead, I'm simply thanking God for guiding me in the right paths this year, for all the right reasons. I've been given the gift of watching my children grow and thrive, had the blessing of my amazing family by my side when life threw curveballs, made amazing new friends, and had the opportunity to come out swinging even harder than I thought I had the capability to.

To every family member and loving friend—may this coming year be filled with the blessings of health and love for all that surrounds you.

Piece by Piece

Clichéd as it always sounds, in what feels like a blink of an eye, our diaper-clad babies begin to emerge from our protective parental cocoon and show us the many ways they are evolving into their own individualistic selves. These are those moments we were once warned about. Unsolicited advice from family, friends, even strangers in the grocery stores who so long ago gazed, with admiration, at our blanketed, bald miracles and warned us not to forget these little moments. Warned (or promised) that the sleepless nights frantically reciting *Love You Forever* by rote would become distant memories. That diaper blowouts, teething nightmares, public temper tantrums, laundering vomit-covered blankets and equally vomit-covered children at 2 a.m.—those would someday be mere, blurry images filed away under the folder heading "Child rearing files I would like to delete and shred."

Every challenging phase we survived in the earliest years was endured with the image within my head of the successful outcomes that were sure to lie ahead. As a lifesaving mantra, I have always tried to talk myself down from the most anguishing ledges by reminding myself that 'This Too Shall Pass." Every moment of self-doubt I had about myself, be it personal or parental, would someday become a part of who my future self would become—like a scattered, manically dumped jigsaw puzzle that, at first glance, looks overwhelming and frankly, not worth the stress. Piece by unique piece, starting from the simpler outside edges and working into the mind-boggling nucleus of my life's puzzle—a beautiful image transformed.

If I were to have fast-forwarded from the placement of that initial moment, when the very first pieces of my puzzle fit together and I had found harmony in the earliest successes, to the "masterpiece" (pausing to, ahem, clear my throat figuratively) that has become a priceless work of art in my world, I wonder how my initial maternal self would have ever believed the mother I somehow grew to be. What would I think of the rough drafting years I spent reading every how-to book on parenting, researching online for every medical piece of advice at the first sign of a sniffle, begrudgingly joining one of those snooty, affluent mother's groups (only to be asked to leave when I just *couldn't* bring myself to make small talk about infant reiki, Swahili 101 for babies, growing and making my own kale and hemp seed nutritional snacks to feed my child's brain—maybe I'm stretching a little—I will save that fun adventure for another time)? Would I ever believe I am sitting here before my screen and bursting with so much adoration and devotion to the beautiful creations who call me "Mom"?

Would I ever have imagined that, just last evening, my little boy would have pulled me aside and inquired about whether or not I would allow him to donate his allowance money to the children in Haiti? All on his own! He explained that last year he had learned of a program called "Hugs for Haiti" that helped out the disastrous number of young children who went without the things our children take for granted. The passion in his voice when he reached out to me to ask for help was overwhelming. I would like to think I had a part in that wonderful child and his compassionate ways toward everyone in the world.

And then, on the third day, August 2005, I created Dylanie. Created, brought forth—either way, she's here to stay. And she's here to provide me with more material than I could ever share with the world.

I learned two valuable lessons last evening, to say the least. I learned that my son will someday change the world in his own ways, with a heart we should all take notes on utilizing.

But that warm and fuzzy moment will end ... *now*.

I also learned that when my eight-year-old daughter asks me to listen to music on my phone, I had better do my homework on her mental playlist. Apparently, as we all do, those little parent *fails* crop up unexpectedly when we are trying to stay hip with our little ones. Heaven knows, I'm exceeding the level of hip mother years in my child's "cool parent cache." Heaven also knows I apparently didn't listen to the lyrics of Kesha's "Timber" in enough depth to know what was about to take place in my living room.

You haven't truly been a mom until your beautiful, eight-year-old daughter belts out the line, "… head down, booty up, timber …" all while putting on quite the performance in her PJs, one that would make Ms. Cyrus proud. Just when I thought I had a hold of this "explaining what is and what isn't appropriate behavior" thing.

I guess it's like anything in life. Parenting is not for the weak of heart, but what a cool job it can be. After all, I'm certainly never bored—or not in need of a tranquilizer dart.

Maybe it wasn't such a terrible thing to get kicked out of a mom's club. What would I *ever* have to write about?

In-Security

So Sean's bringing my two little ones, his little brother and his young cousin to test out their innocent fishing skills at Mill Pond in Somers. Anyone who is familiar with the area and young children will know that the most they are going to catch this time of year is a good time outside with friends. Nobody is expecting to catch dinner or a river monster—just good, old-fashioned fresh air and a meaningful spring experience.

And yes, I realize that opening day for fishing is weeks away. But, let's be human for a moment. They left the house with bread, hotdogs, and Barbie lures as bait. It's kind of a no-brainer and would get them off the hermit technology that traps their little brains inside.

Apparently, as they piled out of the car with excitement, the unofficial and self-appointed Mill Pond security taskforce threatened them as a group that if one child casted a line they would call the Department of Environmental Protection. I'm thinking it was the same elderly gentleman who has given us problems in the past while we were catching and releasing turtles to show my children wildlife in their habitat trying to stick his nosy self into whether or not we had ample life jackets in our kayaks, etc.

Look sir, with all due respect, I have a superior appreciation for the laws and the safety of my family. Furthermore, I have a huge need to allow my children to have every outdoor experience I can squeeze out of nice weather. If your life's ambition is to plant your grumpy geriatric behind day after day and pretend you are the "Paul Blart, Mall Cop" of a sleepy town recreational pond, well then please accept my regards, and best of luck with *that*.

See you after opening day! With my children—and my non-filtered attitude about childhood experiences with the demographics that God gave us to enjoy!

Two-Minute Commute

Here is today's morning commute conversation to daycare with two ADHD-riddled children … verbatim:

Lanie: "Mommy, when I'm a grown-up, will you and daddy and meme and poppa still be alive?"

Me: "You don't need to worry about that."

Lanie: "If you say bad words do you not go to heaven?"

Me: "I'm not sure, but I know it makes God sad."

Lanie: "When I'm a grown-up, will the world run out of houses for sale?"

Me: "I'm sure there will be plenty of houses for you to pick from."

Logan: "Someone on my bus uses bad words."

Me: "That's because they have bad manners. Ignore them."

Logan: "What's your favorite kind of dog?"

Lanie: "Oooh! I see a bird!"

Morbidity, profanity with eternal damnation, real estate, canine preference, and delightful wildlife sightings in a two-mile commute.

My life … I couldn't make this insanity up.

Random Randomness, Part Six, 2015

My life began when I became a mother.
I know that sounds cliché, but it's beyond the truth.
They saved me.

***

Logan asked me what I thought the secret to life was.
Of course, I was without an answer.
But not my little man.
"I think that the secret to life is trying to live it to the fullest
… and maybe fall in love."
Live it up sweet child. Live it like every day is your last.
Sky dive, bungee jump, take chances with a new job, take
chances in general, get that tattoo if it means something to you,
wear plaid with stripes, be polite, hold doors open, cry when
you're sad, laugh when you're happy. Never, ever give up on

yourself, even when giving up sounds *so* much better than persevering.

But falling in love … we need to talk about that one.

She'd better pass *my* tests to be the woman to steal your heart from me.

***

If given a choice between giving a stray cat a bath while simultaneously applying an enema to it or fighting with my daughter in the morning to do her hair—I'd happily choose door number one.

***

Logan (in reference to his little sister): "Mom, you gave birth to a beautiful, creative, not-so-normal nut job!"

Make that two.

Awww … the miracle of sibling adoration.

***

I feel like donkey shit. I don't know a great deal about donkeys, but it sounds about right.

***

No more Spongebob in this house. Ever!

My son just called me to inquire as to what "don't drop the soap" means. He claims he heard it on Spongebob.

After I banged my head against the wall, I asked him to just simply not repeat it at school. Or anywhere else.

***

Can I just go back to bed?

Pulled out of my driveway halfway and got stuck in the ice. Kids in back seat think it's hilarious to hear my tires spin.

Got out and shoveled out the cluster-F behind my tires and wrenched my lower back.

Got back into the car and accidentally uttered the words, "F-ing ridiculous" ... only used the actual term.

Lanie pipes up, "Mom, did you just say "ludicrous"?

"Yes dear, that's what I said."

All of this and I've been awake since 4 a.m.

Tread lightly.

**

And in other news ...

Someone kidnapped my children last night and replaced them with children who are not only cleaning their rooms, but are helping one another clean.

If you have information leading to the retrieval of my original offspring, please disregard.

**

My early morning Wednesday pondering is this: Why must my sweet little girl feel that the backseat of my car is her own personal landfill?

It currently resembles a vortex of forgotten toys lying in wait to meet their own demise in the dumpster when mama finally loses her shit and tosses them away!

**

Girl Scout mom or not, when an adorable, bundled-up, two-front-teeth, blue-eyed-daisy scout rings your doorbell and asks if you want to buy her cookies, *you buy the cookies!*

I'm such a weak sucker for the toothless little ones when they are out practicing their sales skills.

Honestly, she was so precious that, had she been selling used tires, I would have had to open my wallet and not risk seeing disappointment on her sweet little face.

Note: I don't eat cookies. But ... her little mittens and missing teeth.

Sigh ...

Update: So, as I am waist deep in Girl Scout cookies (not eating them, sorting the boxes to deliver), the same adorable blue-eyed little girl rings our doorbell to deliver the cookies that we couldn't resist buying from her.

No lie—she had no front teeth and her winter hat was bigger than her tiny head.

So cute, if she was selling snow, I might have had to put an order in.

***

Taking a quick poll: If someone drove your car the day before and left your gas tank on empty, could you plead insanity in court after you kill the said driver?

Keep in mind I noticed the gaslight on my way to work and had no time to stop.

***

Woke up this morning to an allergy attack so bad that my eyes are red as a baboon's ass. I truly hope nobody thinks I was partying it up on my way to work!

***

Anybody know one of those idiots who decides that their alarm clock is really interfering with their dreams and shuts it off on a workday? You know, the kind that wakes up fifteen minutes before she's supposed to be out the door?

I'd like to introduce myself!

Logan loves to spout random facts about animals, especially cats. Both of my kids are walking encyclopedias when it comes to animals. They both obsessively enjoy reading about different species and breeds and then proceed to impress the hell out of people with their insights and knowledge.

Tonight was not one of those occurrences.

I'm not even sure how tonight's feline fact was gleaned, or gleaned incorrectly, but here it is for your enjoyment.

Logan asked his sister, "What's one thing that the cat species doesn't have that humans have and use to get by with everyday tasks?"

Dylanie didn't skip a beat. In a fraction of a second, without even looking up, she responded, "Buttholes!"

Okay. I'm not gonna lie—I did laugh. However, what kind of bound up, super uncomfortable cats does she read about?

No buttholes?

By the way, the answer was thumbs.

***

That moment when you hear preschoolers randomly blurt out, "Uptown funk you up!" and the second word comes out sounding a tad different.

***

I have found the secret to waking up with gusto in the wee hours of the morning—and it doesn't even involve caffeine!

No, my peeps, all it involves is the unmistakable sound of a cat hacking up vomit in the pitch darkness of a carpeted bedroom at 4:30 am.

There's something about the sound of a cat preparing to throw up in an unknown room in the house that unleashes my gazelle-like speed to find said cat before the inevitable yacking occurs on anything absorbent. An adrenaline rush more powerful than coffee to start my Monday.

I like to feel like my superhero, matrix-like moves leaping out of bed saved my carpet from the wrath of regurgitated Friskies.

This glamorous lifestyle is more than I can take.

***

My children couldn't be more different.

Logan told his sister how much he loved her yesterday and asked why she doesn't tell him the same.

Lanie: "Because you always bother me and try to run my life by telling me what to do!"

Logan: "But can't you just say the words?"

Lanie: "See? You're trying to boss me around!"

So sweet and exasperating all at once.

Wouldn't trade them for the world!

***

Someday, I will look back on these days with gratitude that I was a soccer mom. Today is not one of those days. I just want my PJs and my blankie.

***

Why is it that, when a cashier asks me if I want to donate to a charity when I'm checking out of the store, I feel like such a tool saying no? And, furthermore, besides feeling like a tool saying no (I donate whenever I possibly can, especially if it's a charity for children) I always feel like I owe them an explanation as to why I appear to them like the biggest Scrooge in the world for not donating money to their charity fund raiser. Why?

***

Only in my life:

On the soccer sidelines, my friend points to Logan's shirt and asks if it's a ketchup stain or water.

And we all know, there is no such thing as a lie in our world.

Logan: "It's vomit."

Did I mention he gets carsick?

And he just tells it like it is.

And it wasn't my car!

***

Had to share this because, well, my child is oddly unique and funny as hell.

We were discussing *Sesame Street* characters on the way to daycare. Dylanie tells me that her favorite was Snuffleuphagus (no clue the correct spelling).

I told her I always felt so bad for him because he appeared constantly depressed. I was in mid-sentence when she interrupted. "He's just so blue all the time, he really needs—"

"Allergy medicine!"

Puzzled, I asked why she would say that.

"Mom, have you ever *seen* his eyes?"

I almost drove right off the road laughing.

***

I really do need to relax and stop always worrying about pleasing everyone else. It kind of gets in the way of finding any peace within myself on a daily basis.

***

Today on the beach, I told Lanie to dig to China. She said she didn't want to dig all the way to china because once she got there she wouldn't understand the language

***

Lanie: "Look at my beach hair in the wind Mom! I look like a lion!"

Me: "A beautiful lion at that! It's nice to see your creative views at work on the beach."

Lanie: "Earlier I threw a rock at a seagull!" (Runs off, bounding to the shoreline)

We converse with one another so different in our world.

Hope the seagull fared well.

***

At the arcade tonight, Logan prayed on every quarter: "I'm doing this for my sister … so my sister can pick whatever prize she wants."

I must be doing something right.

Thank you, God, for showing me in dribs and drabs that miracles are always in abundance, in the tiniest of ways, depending on how enormous those tiny ways are perceived.

Thank you for those enormous slaps in my blind perceptions.

I'm doing it right?

Bet your ass I am!

***

Right now, if someone told me they could take away this sinus headache for my left arm, I'd gladly wear my watch on the right.

***

Lets all be the kind of positive change we would want for ourselves today.

Speak kindly, even if it takes a little theatrical attempt.

Give compliments, not criticism. A kind boost seems small, but it can change another person's self-worth immensely.

Smile. Smile a lot. Even if it's the only exercise you get all day.

Love the unlovable. Even the hardest to handle people in our paths need compassion.

Then smile once more!

When the day comes that my time in life is over, I hope that I am remembered for always trying to find the best in others. For being "that girl" who lived to put a smile on a somber face and a laugh that might have somehow made another person's day a little brighter and lighter.

Negative people should have no business trying to rent space in my head. This life is not a competition but, instead, a journey to ride out with love, acceptance, and laughter.

***

Sometimes I stop in my own tracks because the physical world around me is so beautiful that I forget the little, unimportant, not-so-beautiful aspects of everyday life.

***

Just this morning, I was given praise for the positive changes I had brought about within a student's behavior and progress. It wasn't an easy battle to win, and it certainly isn't a perfect science.

Yet, someone whom I admire immensely let me know that my dedication to bettering the life of a young child has not gone unnoticed.

Although it's a part of my job, it feels so amazing to know that my love for those I teach is recognized and that I am not hidden in the background.

***

Sometimes it feels so good to get permission from a trusted friend who gets it to just cry.

Feeling very scared and powerless today. My little boy turns twelve tomorrow and starts middle school in a few weeks.

I know I can't protect him forever. I know the world can be downright cruel.

I know life could be *so* much worse.

But here, in a parking lot on my lunch break—just for now—I need to cry.

***

Watching *Grease* with my daughter never gets old. She's amazed that I know every line and every song verbatim. She's amazed that I had always dreamed of playing Rizzo in an Off-Broadway show.

She's exceptionally surprised that she and I share the same opinion that John Travolta's chin resembles an ass crack.

She's my girl!

***

Today has been one of true self-reflection, dedication, love and appreciation for the most blessed opportunities.

Very glad for tonight being a quiet one to just relax and think about things.

Being an adult is more difficult than I ever imagined.

***

Watching my students getting overly excited about learning today and making life connections to what they have learned is priceless.

Making a mess with last-minute sensory dough and getting caught in a rainstorm together made it that much more fun.

But having one of my little boys wrap his arms around my waist and tell me, "I love you Ms. Trisha!" during a "just because" moment made the day so worthwhile and magical.

I pray that my students understand, when they are too old for "just because" hugs, how much they bring joy into my world every day. Having the gift of being their initial educator as I watch them grasp onto the concepts they will carry with them is worth more than anything monetary.

Here's an imaginary hug to my sweet students, each and every one of them.

I love you more!

***

Why in the actual hell do people in these modern times still use the word "retarded" like it's a staple in their verbal database of ignorant adjectival utterances?

Do these people even have an ounce of class or respect for those around them who might find it truly hurtful?

***

I was just having this conversation with my mother the other day:

Whereas I may often present as flighty, unfiltered, and disorganized, the struggle to get through everyday tasks that are as simple for others as breathing can be like a calculus exam to a third grader. I live a life through daily to-do lists, overthinking, massive anxiety, perpetual motion, and many simple tasks left unfinished.

However, the beauty of my own diagnosis comes to play in being able to understand my own children and their ADHD struggles, the gift of a creative mind that thinks outside of everyone else's "typical" realms of "normal," and a unique, (albeit eccentric) sense of humor.

It took me years to accept that not all who cross my path in life will appreciate or accept the quirkiness that makes me who I am. I choose to view the less tolerant as unfortunate for not seeing the world around them in such a different, colorful life.

Even if their socks always match, and they don't get distracted, mid sentence, by shiny things quite so easily as this girl!

***

Is today a full moon? Wanted to be proactive and reserve a spot in the loony bin before all the vacancies are spoken for by my fellow autism moms and teachers.

I will await your responses while I rock to and fro in my new shiny buckle vest.

***

I'm not going to lie: I'm one of those moms who swears up a storm after she stepped on a Lego.

***

With all the hate going on in the world, I took my mom's advice and paid for the woman behind me at Dunkin' Donuts. My mother likes to do that at least once a week just to prove to a stranger that there is kindness prevalent within this crazy world.

I pray that somehow it put a smile on a stranger's face and that she chooses to pay it forward as well.

In a world where evil is trying to win the battle within mankind, love always wins!

***

When I'm having a tough week and one of my students hugs me and says, "Ms. Twisha, I love that you're my teacher!"

Enough said.

The Purge

"The Purge" is taking place this weekend in my home.

The closet purge.

I'm about to tackle the socks now. I have to accept that the matches will never show up again no matter how many times I do the laundry.

It's awful and therapeutic at the same time. I'm dreading it.

Don't get me started on expensive Victoria's Secret bras that I haven't worn since God knows when. Someone is getting one hell of a donation.

And I finally gave in to the fact that I don't need fifteen pairs of jeans. I literally kept pairs that were the next size up for winter weight gain. Who does that?

I have my outerwear closet next. I refuse to get rid of my obsessive collection of Northface jackets and fleeces.

I got rid of cocktail dresses in the realization that I was never going to be sexy Trisha again.

And because I am a pre-k teacher, everything is casual and comfortable. But matching with Lularoe is so satisfying.

I have a $50 bra from Victoria's Secret that I never wear, but I am keeping it because I'm not a quitter.

Leggings made it hard for any woman to want to lose weight.

Jeans don't lie, but leggings make you believe it's not there!

And God forbid I throw out the professional clothing in case I have the opportunity to interview for a billion-dollar corporation. We all keep that one choice outfit that probably has moth holes in it by now

You never know if Hollywood might call

Yes, I actually parted with shoes.

This is not an easy thing.

Is it really bad if I know that there are matching socks somewhere in the house but throw the pile away out of spite?

And I can't wait to get my hands on the items in my children's rooms that haven't been touched in years. I'm feeling quite evil.

The feeling of ridding my closet of clothes I haven't worn is freeing.

Now, I fear I will be free and naked because I have nothing to wear as the "in case" outfits are bagged and ready to donate.

Be afraid.

I have so many hand-me-downs for my kids that are more expensive than my own clothes.

I did Lanie's closet yesterday and blew through that nonsense like the Tasmanian devil.

Buh-bye extra laundry that she wears for an hour and throws on the floor.

Lanie has no clue that I diminished her wardrobe by three-fourths. And I give zero cares.

My son is so small for fourteen, but some of his shirts were jacked up and needed to go be at peace elsewhere.

It's sad when you realize that you live in leggings, hoodies, T-shirts, and Nikes.

But now I need pretty shoes to fill the empty space.

Dustpan

A glimpse of my chaotic Saturday morning:

Making my children do manual labor by cleaning the living crap out of their bedrooms. I told them anything not cleaned and put away will be tossed in the trash by their evil mom (aka, *me!* Bwahaha!).

Logan was off-the-chart OCD about what to keep and what to toss—perseverating to the tenth degree.

My anxiety was at nut-house level. I needed a release, something to bring me back to modified bat-shit-crazy level.

In other words, back to feeling myself.

And my daughter, in a sobbing, whining, complaining, mom-hating frenzy came storming out with a dustpan, demanding to know where the trash was.

The dustpan contained one sparkly shoe, her headbands, books, socks, framed pictures, and various other items of random nature.

Me: "Why would you choose to throw out things you obviously need and like?"

Dylanie: "Because you've made me too angry to pick it up so I'm throwing it away!"

Umm … Am I the only one who sees the oxymoronic irony in her hormone-induced actions?

Me: "Okay, here's the trash. Go nuts!"

As she stomped back to her room, I retrieved the books, pictures, and shoe.

I can't let my love for early literacy and cute shoes be insulted in such an act of travesty.

Plus, the framed picture had me in it, and I looked cute.

As an added bonus, Logan then lay on his bedroom floor with a blue bin on his head complaining that all of his cleaning was causing him to have low blood sugar.

God how I wish I could make this up.

Candy

I will preface this with the fact that today was a day for the books containing crappy days.

I drove home tonight feeling as though I didn't even have the energy to deal with my own kids—and that really sucks considering what I do for work. My energy should be driven by a maternal need to shower my kids with my complete and undivided attention. But I was spent and empty.

When I picked up my beautiful creations, somehow my heinous day dissolved into my past, never to be brought back to the surface.

Now I will warn you, I have a story for you all. One of my "out of the mouths of Muller children" kind of stories. But alas, I am beyond the throes of exhaustion and in need of a shower to wash the "gifts" that my students expel on me daily, as working in preschool has a little added bonus.

I need to share the highlight of my day. After the storm comes the rainbows, right?

My son, for many reasons, cannot have food with artificial dyes. That's difficult enough when it comes to a normal daily diet, but it plain *sucks* during valentines when every damn Valentine has to contain a trinket just brewing and pulsating with artificial dyes!

He's a little boy who accepts that he can't enjoy the treats that arise from this God-forsaken Hallmark holiday.

But I've done something right with my children. For every tear, fear, panic, and doubt I've experienced raising these two beings, I have succeeded in creating such nice little people.

Currently, my son is making piles of the candy that he will never enjoy—candy that most kids his age would already have been devoured and become a distant memory.

He is proudly declaring that these piles of candy will go to his little sister and our good friends and neighbors. Candy that he accepts that he cannot enjoy yet wants others to enjoy.

And he is proud to give it away. My heart doesn't hurt for whatever he can't do, but rather is swelling with pride at a wonderful little man that I had something to do with.

And you know what? He's *not* going without. This mom decided that that *each* piece of candy he will not enjoy will be reciprocated with extra time on the Xbox—something I never do.

But I will this time.

Because, well, what *is* life without equal parts sacrifice and pleasure?

Safe

I had to run my car for an hour to get it to heat up and melt most of the ice that was covering the entire car. Then, because my car was running for an hour, my gas light came on, so I had to stop and get gas. Then I had to drive to work going no more than thirty miles an hour the entire way because the roads were treacherous. People kept honking at me and flipping me off. The best part of my nightmare commute was when I saw my life flash before my eyes. Because the roads were so icy, I was nearly plowed into by a huge truck that lost control and spun out barely missing me by two feet. It's too bad that I was already going to be late for work because I would love to tend to the heart attack I'm sure I was having from the experience and would also love to change my pants because I'm pretty sure I almost crapped myself.

On the bright side, at least I'm going to work so that I can make enough money to pay for the gas that I just put into my car (that I had to let run for an hour to warm up) to get to work.

To all drivers who found themselves behind me on my morning commute today: tailgating me will only result in me driving even slower. My safety and getting home to my family in one piece today is more important than your need to show me your dangerous, ignorant need to drive like an ass in the snow. Pass me, lay on your horn, bang on your steering wheel, and flip me off all you want. To paraphrase Frank Sinatra, "I drove it my wayyyyyy."

By the way, hit my car and I can promise you that you will be a lot more irate when I sue your impatient behind.

Please take my advice. If you don't have to be on the roads stay home. It's not worth it to risk your life. When I tell you the roads are like a skating rink I am not exaggerating. Stay safe, everyone.

A lot of people might judge me for my fear of driving in the snow and ice.

In 2009, I was working in Windsor as an educator and lost control of my SUV on an icy road. I was driving well below the speed limit because of the icy roads. I swerved to avoid a telephone pole and hit a tree instead. My children's booster seats were in the front seat and dashboard when I woke up from being knocked unconscious from the airbag. My son's seatbelt was literally snapped apart.

I had dropped them off at daycare not ten minutes prior to the accident.

Ten minutes.

The conditions that I was driving in at the time were trivial compared to today's weather.

I walked away with a broken nose, facial burns, and a slipped disk. I was extremely lucky.

The image of the booster seats wedged into my front seat and dashboard will forever haunt me.

Please be safe. Nothing in this world is worth chancing a human life.

Ten minutes prior …

Expectations and Destinations

Not everyone is so lucky to be chosen to take the different paths in life like an autism parent travels.

True, they are paths that the "What to Expect" books will never touch on in the lives we have been bestowed.

For there aren't books that can ever prepare us "chosen parents" for the "expectations" that come with the unknown, sometimes frightening paths that we have no choice but to attempt to follow.

Our paths are often littered with routes that are suddenly detoured into unfamiliar territories. Our shortcuts during our rides are frequently and without warning, "under construction," or "delayed for miles."

There are unexpected potholes and slippery turns. There are traffic jams and those who travel alongside us who will cut us off as they don't realize we are traveling lost with our hazards flashing, looking for safe places to pull over and find answers.

But ... the scenery during the journey! The alternate paths that lead us to places we didn't see coming on our "GPS." The destinations that took twice the fuel and mileage to arrive at but took our breath away when we *finally* got there.

I'm forever grateful that the map I once believed was my key to a smooth journey as a mother was, in fact, a map to oblivion. The fact that I have been lost so many times trying to get to the "correct" destination has given me a course in defensive driving and has forced me to stop, stretch my legs, and embrace the routes to an amazing place.

A place that exists in the soul of the miracle little boy that I created.

I love my road trips!

Random Randomness, Part Seven, 2016

Playing Trivial Pursuit with my kids and I ask my daughter a history question: "What were jeans first called?"

When your ten-year-old chooses "booty chokers" or "banana hammocks" as her final answers, one doesn't know whether to laugh, cry or face palm …

True story.

***

I suppose I should get out of my dirty jammies and shower to put on clean jammies.

***

Sometimes it's nice to not feel so alone in such a dark struggle. If I could reach out and let one person know that I am holding their hand theoretically through this journey, and I have done my job.

***

If I won Powerball, I would give my family the world and still choose to live simply.

All the money in the world can't replace the feeling in helping others find solitude and live without worry in the world.

By the way, I don't buy tickets. I don't ever want to chance having the means to replace true happiness with something monetary.

But if I did win, my mom, dad, brother, children, family, friends, and charities would experience a lifetime of peace and no worries.

That's what our journey in life is meant for.

***

That moment when your student's parent messages you to tell you that their child got into the car after school and told her, "Ms. Trisha really, really rocks.!"

That moment. You rock too, my sweet buddy!

***

My daughter is such a younger me!

I went in to check on her because she was quiet (to make sure she wasn't torturing the cats by plastering them down with hundreds of feminine products for sheer pleasure—this is a true story for another day).

I was pleasantly surprised and experiencing slight déjà vu when I saw her reading a chooser chapter book by the minuscule light from her peace-sign night light. Brought back fond memories of me doing the same while I learned the facts of life through a great literary legend: Ms. Judy Blume.

My old, trusty nightlight sat at my side during the initial knowledge intake regarding boobies, boy's unmentionable pubescent occurrences, and what "making out" was really about.

Yeah … hmmmmmmmmmmmmmmmm.

My daughter is reading *Diary of a Wimpy Kid* or something equally academically enhancing.

At least I have a day or two before she learns of the topics we had to read about as innocent youth.

***

Between the new vocabulary my son is learning in middle school and what is overheard by both of my children from my favorite radio station in the morning, I am really batting .100 lately raising my children properly.

Mind you, they can't hear me screaming like a bat-shit crazy lunatic in the morning to get ready for school. However, somehow they don't miss the inappropriate utterances that make me want to hang my head in shame when they inquire their meanings.

Happy Friday to all the parents reading this who did not almost drive off the road after being questioned by a ten- and twelve-year-old about the definitions of both a "shart" *and* a "skin flute."

***

That day that you mistaken your daughter's pants for your own and wear them to work. I'm feeling like a quart in a pint container.

***

So this happened while having a conversation with my son on the drive to school this morning (right after he solved the Rubik's cube seven times during a six-minute commute, I might add).

"Buddy, why do you choose to sit by yourself at the front of the bus every day? Don't you ever want to chat with some of your friends?"

"I don't mind my own company. That's what makes me an introvert. Sometimes I choose to be passive instead of assertive. Plus, it saves me from having to listen to the ignorant cursing from the kids who I'd rather not have a conversation with"

Aspie logic win! He makes me so speechless at times. Love that child with all that I am.

***

Sometimes when the reality of my world truly brings me down, I take a drive to buy my daughter Motrin at 8:30 at night for two reasons:

1. To buy my daughter Motrin because she has a headache and I'm a really good mom.

2. Because I'm a really good mom and I need to escape so that I can scream and cry without my children knowing a mother would do such a thing.

I would give anything if it meant that my children's lives could be easier.

Just feeling very blue tonight and I'm allowing myself to do so because I don't have the answers that moms should be able to have when their children's world is a struggle.

I often tell myself that it could be so much worse and that I am truly blessed for what I have in this world. However, tonight I am allowing myself to be selfish and angry that my child needs something that I just can't make easy.

I think we would all be a lot better if we gave ourselves the opportunity to cry once in a while when we don't understand God's plan.

***

What is it about buying cute undies from Victoria's Secret that has such healing powers?

***

I love my children with every piece of my heart and soul.

It's a good thing that I cherish my role as a mother.

The hormonal, preteen, whining attitude that I experienced this morning helped me to empathize with the reasonings as to why some animals eat their young.

To be fair, I *was* asking a little too much of her by suggesting she put a sweatshirt on when she complained that it was too cold outside.

And the fact that I wouldn't let her steal the orange and pink balloons off the drive-thru sign at Dunkin Donuts really takes my mother of the year tiara away.

***

I just want to believe that the good people on earth far outshine the monsters who don't believe in loving their neighbors.

***

If you know me, you know I wouldn't ever turn down a beach opportunity.

But tomorrow is supposed to be as hot as the Devil's soul and I just can't fathom the idea of watching the ocean with sweat in my eyeballs.

To the ocean, I apologize. It's not you. It's me.

***

Once in a while, the natural beauty surrounding us makes me forget that the world can seem so full of negativity to many of us far too often.

Stop, breathe, and find the subtle signs.

We are all stuck together on this Earth for a limited time.

Find the beauty in the sunsets, accept the storms, smile when it feels impossible, and tell someone daily one thing to lift her up.

Be that change you want to see in the world.

We are all we've got. Let's give it our best while we still are blessed to share it with someone whose day we may change with a mere smile.

***

I've heard the saying that behind every successful parent and is a parent who is positive they're screwing their child up.

If that doesn't ring true for me lately, I don't know what the truth is. I can't stand this running around nonstop for my children's extracurricular activities and not ever spending time with my children.

I am so over this adult thing. I need to hide in a corner with my blankie and have somebody tell me it's going to be Okay.

***

Oh, dear God, why do I ever have to even *think* that I will be having this conversation?

Can't they stay five?

I don't want to talk about … ahem … erections with my baby boy. I don't even like the word.

I'm so sending him to his dad for those choice talks. Best of luck with that.

***

Yesterday, Sean made a gigantic pot of French onion soup. Needless to say, besides the fact that everyone's eyes were watering from the abundance of onions and spices, it was amazing.

However, today my clothes reeked of yesterday's cuisine no matter how much I tried to mask it.

One of my students sat next to me and said, "Miss Trisha, you smell so good today, just like a sausage dinner."

Not quite the fragrance that I would like to be remembered for.

***

Men will never understand the pressure that women are under to just look human.

***

Today is such a special day.

Today is the anniversary of two amazing people who took their wedding vows beyond anything imaginable. In sickness and in health, through good times and bad, my parents have never been anything less than the best of friends and each other's soulmates.

My parents are the example of the most amazing love and dedication that two people could have for one another when life became real. When the memories of the best of times were often shadowed by the most trying and scary times.

Happy anniversary mom and dad! You are both the biggest heroes and inspirations in my world. Thank you for showing the world that true love is based on friendship and undying faith and strength.

Love you more.

***

It's during the most heart-wrenching days that I need to stop and take in the innocent beauty of my sleeping children. The two babies who blessed my world with a belief that God has to be amazing to have allowed me to create two little people who saved my life.

However, God, if we could just have coffee together one day, I have a few questions and favors to ask of you.

***

I need to start to appreciate the things in my life I take for granted every day. I have learned this weekend how much tomorrow is not a guarantee, but a gift.

Sing out loud to the music, even if you are tone deaf. Eat what you are craving, even if it's not on your daily menu. Color your hair blue if it makes you happy, regardless of the looks you might get from those who don't understand. Buy the shoes, even if they aren't on sale. Get that tattoo you've always dreamed about. People will get over it.

Tell them how much you love them ... even if it feels awkward.

Then, tell them again.

***

An amendment was added to the ever-growing list of direct orders I never thought I would have to give to my children.

"Under no circumstances will you play truth-or-dare with your brother and dare him to touch the cat's butt hole!"

Folks, as if this wasn't a horrifying and necessary amendment to the list, be advised that I had to enforce this new rule as it was not an isolated incident.

I don't know who looks more ashamed, the sixteen-year-old deaf cat or me.

***

Going grocery shopping on an empty stomach. If I'm not heard from in a few days, call the authorities.

***

That moment when you are inspecting your cucumber in the grocery store and a creepy man is watching you.

And doesn't have a cart or basket to prove that he is shopping.

***

Me (to my kids actually getting along): "I love the fact that you two are literally the best of friends and sometimes enemies. You wouldn't know what to do with yourselves without each other"

Logan: "If you think about it, it's like the theory of a single celled amoeba really."

Me: *crickets chirping*

Me: "Just eat your McNuggets and … yeah … just clean up when you're finished."

This kid will definitely make sure my nursing home is comparable to the Ritz.

He's going to make so much money and be so successful as an adult.

Until then, I have no idea how he makes intelligent connections to my words. He's smarter than I could ever be at 13.

And what's the story with these amoebas anyway?

***

I am not making this up.

There are silver linings everywhere when you least expect them.

I was feeling really kind of blue today. I wasn't sure how to shake it.

Then, one of my students came up to me at naptime, kissed my cheek, and said, "Ms. Trisha, will you sing Hallelujah quietly with me? I love it when we sing our favorite song together."

And just like that, that blue feeling turned a little more purple.

We sang it twice. Out of tune and with all of the beautiful innocence that comes with a child's amazing way of making the wrong lyrics so sweet and uplifting.

I love the simplest moments.

The Effing F-Word

Like all parents, we strive to the best of the abilities we know to be role models for our children. We teach everything from the importance of appearance and hygiene, to manners and respect. The list is infinite and often intricate, so I won't go further with examples. If you are a said role-modeler parent, you get what I referring to.

I am no exception to this rule. I was raised and continue to raise by the principles in life that state the parenting 101 rules for modeling and helping my own children grow up knowing to respect their peers and elders, use manners (even if it's overkill), have self-respect enough so that others will see you as a strong member of society with much to offer our fellow associates.

And yada, yada. The point I am trying to convey is this: I try. Really and truly, I try. I figure I have borrowed time in these delicate years to pound these simple yet crucial human qualities into those two precious craniums before I have teenagers and their brains develop that emergency shut off switch that comes inevitably factory stocked when it comes to their parents' attempts at guidance.

In layman's terms, before I go from being the hero in their lives and morph into the embarrassing, nagging other person who lives in their house and plots ways to ruin their lives by still writing their names on their lunch bags, or tries to convince their friends to check out my 80s hair band cassette collection, complete with the Monster Ballads box set I ordered in '98 because, well, just because I could jam out to every song in my old Saturn—and I was damn hot doing it.

So to get back to where I began before I start belting out "Every Rose Has It's Thorn," I have always tried to curb my foul, questionable language when in the company of my children. It seemed to come naturally, as though my oral filter went into immediate autopilot the second they walked through the door.

Oral filter … (snickering).

The "F-bomb" is the proverbial no-no around my kids and I have never shied away from calling others out when that monster rolled, unknowingly, off their tongues when my kids were in earshot. I would be lying to all of you if I were to say it didn't roll (tumble, sashay, cartwheel) out of my own mouth far too easily around close friends when those few and far between "adult gatherings" took place. I would be lying to you if I said it wasn't my favorite curse word. Let's face it, when said with a vengeance, we become pretty badass in our own minds. And there are just certain times when "stinkin', freakin', dastardly" just aren't gonna cut it.

But never around my children.

Until yesterday.

I guess I left this trinket of information out, as I was revelling in the glorious moments that came after the dreaded mommy "utterance." I was too busy being flooded with gratitude and adoration for the ability to spend such a much needed outing together, just my sweet angels and their mother—a mother who, in my children's eyes, only speaks in positive prose and finds the rainbows after the storms.

And suddenly, an SUV whose driver apparently didn't see my Camry bouncing like it had hydraulics with two excited children pressed against their windows like those old Garfield window cling-ons from the 80s, threw itself into reverse, NASCAR style, nearly taking out the front end of my car—the front end where the blinker had been patiently blinking as we waited Brady Bunch style for our adventure.

Fearing for our safety and in a frantic knee-jerk reaction, my 1950s mother persona rolled away and disappeared like the party favor-like shoes of the crushed Wicked Witch of the East. Horn blaring, knuckles whitened around the steering wheel, it happened.

"Are you effing crazy, lady!?"

And then can the pause, so silent I could here my own fingernails growing. And I knew there was no going back.

Logan: "Mom! Clean your litter box!"

Dylanie: "Oooh, Mom said the *real* bad word!"

And I couldn't deny it. I wouldn't deny it. In my mind, at that moment, I knew I had crossed a line that I could never erase. Mind racing, I knew I had just solidified future years of their therapies, turned them into future criminals. Their grades would begin to fail, cults formed. I had erased all the good I had done for ten years. I would never be the mother they once looked at with big, adoring eyes.

I was now *that* mother.

So I attempted damage control. It was my only lifeline, my only life jacket in a sea of sharks.

Me: "You are both absolutely right. That was a *terrible* word and I should have known better."

Tick tock. Endless three seconds. I awaited their response.

Dylanie: "Can we get popcorn and sour patch kids inside?"

Well, that was a dastardly, freakin' crazy bullet I dodged.

Did I mention how much my kids put me in my place in so many ways?

It's a really good place, too.

Don't you Know Me?

Every week that my daughter goes to the library, she checks out books on every breed, category, shape, size, color, etc. of various animals. She lives, breathes, eats, sleeps, and dreams about animals. I've always been in awe of her unending knowledge of every nonhuman creature that walks the earth.

So today, during our ride home from the library, she was talking about every type of dinosaur known to man, complete with intricate details. She had returned five library books on last week's canine flavor choices of the week and had checked out five more books on prehistoric beasts. I made a comment about how I knew she would go so far in life because of her passion for animals. I made the suggestion that one day she might become a veterinarian. She threw herself back in horror, as though my words burned her. She asked me to please never wish that on her future again. When I asked why that idea was so undesirable to her, she answered. And I couldn't keep the laughter in.

"Why would you ever even say such a thing! Don't you know me? Don't you know how much I love eating meat?"

Perhaps I should curb her desire to learn about the animal world and tutor her on correct vocabulary terms and meanings that are often mistaken for one another.

Trading Places

I have to share this. I won't sleep if I don't.

Lanie: "Mom, this summer, can we take an extra vacation and visit heaven!"

Me: "You know that's impossible. Heaven is a magical place and no one we can simply visit."

Lanie: "But I want to ask God for a special request."

Me: "What's your request?"

Lanie: "Ugh, now I can't remember."

Logan: "Is it world peace?"

Lanie: "No."

Logan: "Oh, because world peace always works."

Lanie: "Oh, I remember! I wanted to ask God if you and me could trade places for one day."

Me: "Why do you want to trade places?"

Lanie: "So I can work with all those babies and be a grown-up."

Me: "Don't wish your life away. Enjoy being a kid. Being an adult isn't too much fun."

Lanie: "Oh, it will be fun for me. When I'm an adult I'm gonna own a zoo or be a dog caregiver or own a daycare."

Logan: "You said you would work for me when you were a grown-up. Besides, I'm gonna need you when I have to take care of kids because I don't know how to do it."

Me: "I didn't know how until I became your Mom. It's something you learn as you go."

Logan (looks at his sister): "I'm gonna need your help"

Mommy Fail

My son needed help with his math homework. Anyone who knows me understands that math is a weakness for me. I loathe math. All through college, I feared ever having to educate young learners about the world of mathematics because, quite frankly, I felt sorry for said young learners.

Anyway, the question in his homework asked about converting milliliters into liters and how the answer was found.

I was having a brain fart in regards to conversions, so I turned to the most logical source for assistance: I went online and asked Siri.

Being that Logan is Logan—well, this was what he decided was an honest, logical answer. To answer the homework question, "How did you find your answer?" which I'm sure was supposed to be an explanation of the math involved, Logan wrote, "We went online and asked Siri."

Logan is painfully honest.

Thank *God* I went back over his homework with him before it was handed in.

P.S. I promise you I had left the room before resorting to outside, online help. He may not act like he's listening sometimes, but he has sonic hearing abilities and overheard my online query from the next room.

Enjoy a chuckle over my "tail between my legs" moment.

From the Chronicles of
"A Bedtime Routine in the Life of Trisha Muller"

In the first bedroom …

Logan: "What am I going to do someday when I don't have you or dad to rub my back at night?"

Heart-warming and tear-inducing. (Not going to admit that I told him that I would commute to do it throughout adulthood if his future wife understood the mom/son bond.) My heart melts so much with how much love he spreads.

In the second bedroom …

Dylanie: "By accident, I hit the cat in the balls when I was playing with him. Do you think it hurts worse to get hit in the penis or the ballsack if you're a cat? If it's by accident."

crickets

Yeah. So …

Thank you for joining us for, "A Bedtime Routine in the Life of Trisha Muller."

Now run as far away as you can—especially those with preteen girls.

If not, your bedtime stories are about to be replaced with phallic inquiries and heartache.

Just run. Thank me later.

Much love and peace to all!

Claws Out

I will premise this endearing gem of a story with the promise that I am not a violent person. I'm quite pleasant. And funny. But if you mess with my kids something awful awakens within me.

Dylanie told me yesterday that another child has been punching multiple children on her school bus this past week. Of course, immediately I ask her if this child had touched her in any way. She told me, somewhat to the relief of my inner mother bear instincts, that this child never physically hurt her, but rather kept telling her how "stupid" she was on a daily basis.

Oh really? So, folks, I'm not gonna lie. Claws out, fangs exposed, I was already reveling in the fantasy of phone calls to the school, bus company, this child's parents—to, I don't know, get justice? Threaten? Force this child to tell my little girl that he had made one hell of a hiccup in her self-confidence, along with the self-confidence of the other little children he had bullied?

I was pissed and seeing red. Nobody has a right to make another child fearful to participate in the childhood rite of passage that is the school bus ride—especially when you attack my child, verbally or physically.

But something happened that changed me at that moment and probably for the rest of my life. My son. My sweet, shy, non-confrontational, introverted, and loving little boy spoke up. His words? "Don't worry, Dylanie, because I will ride your bus with you and tell him he's the stupid one."

Up until yesterday, "stupid" wasn't allowed to be uttered in our home. My Logan took the big brother approach and wanted to protect his little sister. He's all of sixty pounds and comes up to my rib cage. He sleeps with a nightlight and still needs me to rub his back at night.

But at that moment, the pride I felt in watching my son's empathy towards his little sister—there are some things I can only explain to you in writing, but I know you will never truly feel it.

I never did call the bus company. Logan's got this, at least in theory.

Random Randomness, Part Eight, 2017

I can't tell you how excited I am to go into work today during the beginning of a full moon on Friday the 13th.

The excitement is comparable to prepping for a colonoscopy while brushing my teeth with a cactus.

A turbo shot in my coffee this morning is a harsh necessity.

To all my fellow teachers, may the odds truly be in your favor today.

***

Proudest mommy moment in the most recent past happened this evening.

Sang "Hey Jude" almost in harmony with my daughter tonight in the car after Girl Scouts. Following that, she asked me to teach me about the lives of each member of the Beatles. Being that I am a late-70s baby, I guess I will need to do my research to bring her up to speed. But, goddamnit, I will do my best! That's my girl!

There is hope for her, perhaps.

We can do this.

***

I'm compiling a list of things I would like to receive for my 40th birthday. Here they are in no particular order.

1. A Costco-sized injection of Botox. Maybe two in case the first one doesn't make the cut.

2. A 10-hour, full-body massage with snacks

3. A five-year connection with a house cleaner who doesn't mind coming by every day.

4. A month-long Caribbean cruise or an all-inclusive stay at a resort somewhere tropical.

5. Someone to come to my house every day and make sense of my hair in the morning while they get my kids dressed and fed for school.

Anyone interested, you have a little over two months to get on the ball. Thank you for your time and consideration to this matter.

***

No he didn't.

Just got home from Boy Scouts and told Logan to change out of his uniform and brush his teeth.

His response?

"You're killin' me, Smalls"

Is this child for real?

To add to tonight's humor, my daughter stated, "Mom, you're so petite and you don't scare me anymore because I'm almost as tall as you and can pop your behind a lot faster because you're so short so you can't run as fast as me."

Honey, do you not know how things work in this house? She scooted her skinny behind to bed really fast after she made her statement known.

I will pop that girl's behind when she's 70 if she needs it, and if I'm not six feet under.

They are learning that I am not all about being a cool mother.

They are also learning that I don't play around when I want something done.

Petite that, my little spawns.

***

I have lived 40 years to be able to have bragging rights.

How did I get so lucky to have such a beautiful family?

***

I don't think any of us realize the impact that we make within the lives of others. We too often think we are minuscule second thoughts.

How beautiful would it be to see the impact we make in the lives of those around us in life, rather than never know how moved others are by our mere existences when our chapters come to a close?

***

In the end, our lives are not about the end of our story, but the really good stuff that made our journeys amazing. The times filled with laughter, tears, friendship, and love. That's the part of our story that makes our lives live on eternally.

***

Please, sleep fairy, have some understanding and let me shut my brain off.

This is going to be a long-ass night and a longer-ass day tomorrow if I can't find a nice agreement with my eyelids.

***

My daughter is going to make me rock in a padded corner with a shiny vest.

***

As a mother and a human being, I try very hard not to judge others. However, with that being said, I need to ask why some men feel the need to wear spandex bathing suits at the beach? (Using the term "bathing suit" is being kind). I understand that some women wear a bathing suit that leaves little for the imagination, but when a man in his 60s has on a sheath of stretchy material that quite clearly shows his Frank and man-berries through the outline, it makes it a little uncomfortable. Especially when it's my eleven-year-old daughter that pointed the ghastly scene out first before I could even shield her preteen eyes away.

***

Officially calling BS on SPF. I have literally layered my children and myself at least 10 times a day with SPF 50.

On the plus side, I am half Irish and this could be a lot worse.

However, unless I wear a tarp and a ghillie suit, I am doomed with tan lines.

I remember the days when I was little and we could get away with SPF 8 and come home with those cute little white behinds.

Not so cute anymore when there's no ozone layer and Botox costs a fortune.

***

Even when on vacation, it's so much fun to find treasures from the ocean to share with my students when we explore our ocean thematic unit. I have had way too much fun finding all kinds of things for them to have hands on learning experiences.

I love that I'm such a nerd.

***

Nothing says sibling love like burying your big brother in the sand and then using him as a soccer goal post.

No. For real.

***

Anyone want to do two and a half loads of sandy laundry for me and grocery shop for my bare refrigerator?

No?

... begins weeping.

***

Whatever I ate before I went to bed caused me to have nonstop dreams about consoling Chandler from *Friends* because he had a singing career opportunity and had to have his voice box removed.

All damn night.

***

I love the reminder from my Fitbit to get ready to go to sleep.

Learn me, you glorified fitness monitoring swatch watch. I've got nightly overthinking to do. I'm not your wench. Worry about your damn self.

***

Filling up a piñata for my kid's birthday party has me realizing that sticking handfuls of candy into a donkey's ass is no easy task.

***

The wasp that decided to sting me while I was gardening needs to know … I will find you and I will kill you.

***

I honestly wish I had the opportunity to volunteer in Texas after the latest hurricane. Regardless of what they would need, anything I could do is better than watching these poor people who have lost everything. So devastating.

Sometimes, we need to understand that our most devastating times are moot compared to what others are suffering through.

***

Hello God, it's me, Trisha.
I take back wanting to be an adult.
If you can help a girl out, I'll be on my best behavior.
Okay, we know *that's* never going to happen.
Can I at least get an immunity plea?

***

So happy to be home with my kids. Even though it's time to tuck them in, I truly embrace these moments. I love my babies even when they drive me insane at bedtime.

However …

Cannot wait to wash off today and get under my blanket. Time to turn off my brain and actually rest.

Please brain … please have pity on my need for sleep.

***

Damn, my babies need to stop in time and stay little. They are growing faster than I am ready to allow. They're both supposed to be my preemie miracles forever. Super tiny, bald, and swaddled tight on my chest.

I did not sign up for the preteen/teen bonus round.

***

You know what makes tonight so special?

Aside from sleeping a total of seven hours the past two nights, hospital shit, throwing my back out yesterday and dying in agony all day, not having even the essentials in the house to even make a meal comprised of condiments and despair, washing soccer uniforms at 8 p.m., only to find I was missing one of her socks.

The fun came from going into my car to get my phone charger and thinking a rotting carcass had found its resting place within.

No, no! That would be her missing, gnarly soccer sock.

Silver lining: at least I know she got a good and sweaty practice in tonight for this weekend's tournament.

See? I can be a positive roll of toilet paper in a shit storm after all!

Sweet dreams and peace to everyone.

Tomorrow is a full moon.

***

Can someone at least drop a winning lottery ticket in a parking lot where I might pass through? Shit, drop a $5 and I will be elated at this point.

***

My girl has a fractured ankle and it is close enough to the growth plate on her fibula that she gets to rock an air boot and crutches for four weeks. Then, the crutches can be eliminated.

162

Stick an effing fork in me. I'm just numb to shit news lately.

Just thankful that it was minor. I'm so devastated that her soccer season will have to end early. She's so pissed that she can't finish the season.

We are a family of pissed people lately.

**

I have always advocated for a more positive world. I love to make people smile and laugh when life makes life decisions.

Everyone has off days.

Here's my off-day quote:

"Eff-you life and you're shitty choices for the good people. If you're trying to make us strong, we get it. We've fought your fight far too long. Give us a damn break before you break the ones who believed in believing."

Please.

Give us a break. We've been strong for far too long.

It's not a contest. We all come into the world and leave it at some point.

I'm not asking for too much. Just stop making it so hard to put one foot in front of the other.

I don't want to be rich. I just need you to see that we've had enough.

We've had enough.

**

I keep having dreams about a beautiful country valley called "Route 157." I need to do some research about the meaning of the number.

**

I hope I'm never as much of a bat-shit mess as Winona Ryder in *Stranger Things.*

***

A helicopter mom is one who is constantly obsessed with the well-being and safety of her child. It's to a point of all consuming and likened to the kind who would be okay with wrapping them in bubble wrap and putting a 24-hour surveillance on them.

That ain't me.

Everyone has Privates

Okay. My experience surprising the kids with hopping off the school bus and heading to the movies was a great success. Superior in every way. Even I found the movie to have its moments of adult naughty humor, which generated the sick and immature innate part of my being. I love adult naughty humor.

So, with that being said, the conversation with my little girl en route to the movies this afternoon (as our conversations always are) was both highly entertaining and one that rendered my breathing rather shallow.

"Mom, know what? Today I had library and I was reading a "cycloponia" … (which, I gather, and I could be wrong, is what we neurotypicals refer to as an "encyclopedia") … "and there was something *so* disgusting inside."

Me: "What were you reading about?"

My daughter, if you met her, is not one to *ever* speak in a level below sonic boom, so the fact that she attempted to meekly muster up a hushed voice at this point has already got me on edge.

Dylanie: "It talked about S-A-X glands *and* it showed pictures of them."

Yes, she actually spelled it out. Well friends, I do like to consider myself well educated, worldly, and fine tuned to many aspects in life that others may not be on board with. Intrigued, I pressed further about this foreign topic provided to my baby girl, courtesy of the library's "cycloponia."

Me: "What, may I ask, is an S-A-X gland?"

Have I not learned my lesson enough with this child? If Dylanie says something inappropriate, then one simply does *not* press further for information.

Dylanie: "Can I say the word if I tell you what I saw?"

And I actually said yes. Call it slipping out if my mouth, call it morbid curiosity. I said yes.

Dylanie: "It was about sex glands and it showed pictures of, you know, privates. It was so gross!"

So I tried to be the cool/laid back/matter-of-fact mom in my response. I have always believed that my children should be able to talk to me about anything without shame. Not in a friend sense, but in a safe haven maternal sense.

Me: "Well, Lanie, face it. Everyone has privates. Not a big deal."

Easy enough. Quick and simple response. Move forward.

Nope. It didn't end there. But it ended so well. So damn well.

Dylanie: "Well, I don't care. I think privates are gross, especially when they show boy privates."

Ding, ding, ding! We have a winner! Score! (But not until you're at least thirty-five.)

Keep that way of thinking, beautiful little girl. I knew I was doing something right! What a beautiful end to a week, all thanks to a gross picture in a public school's "cycloponia."

Quiz Time

Without prompting, ask your child these questions and write *exactly* what they say about you:

Logan, age fourteen, Dylanie, age twelve:

What is something I say a lot? Logan: "I love you!" Dylanie: "I'm gonna pow-pop you on the butt."

What makes me happy? Logan: "When you see your children happy." Dylanie: "Coming home to something nice and when we're in a good mood."

What makes me sad? Logan: "When I know that other people aren't happy." Dylanie: "When I yell at Logan."

How tall am I? Logan: "About 4'11". Or maybe 5"." Dylanie: "5'2"."

What's my favorite thing to do? Logan: "Make sure everyone is happy." Dylanie: "Hang out with our family."

What is my favorite food? Logan: "Salad." Dylanie: "Lobster."

What is my favorite drink? Logan: "Coffee." Dylanie: "Powerade."

If I could go anywhere, where would I go? Logan: "Straight somewhere with us." Dylanie: "Maine."

Do you think you could live without me? Logan: "No. Never." Dylanie: "No!"

How do I annoy you? Logan: "When you argue." Dylanie: "That you won't give me a makeup lesson."

What is my favorite TV show? Logan: *"Friends."* Dylanie: *"Stranger Things."*

What is my favorite music to listen to? Logan: "Country." Dylanie: "Country, yo!"

What is my job? Logan: "You're a child-care provider." Dylanie: "You're a pre-k teacher!"

How old am I? Logan: "Forty." Dylanie: "Forty."

What's my favorite color? Logan: "Purple." Dylanie: "Purple."

How much do you love me? Logan: "To the moon and back." Dylanie: "On a scale from one to ten, eleven!"

Gonna be a *Fantastic Day* (Insert Sarcasm)

Didn't set the alarm and woke up at 6:40. No shower, no breakfast, funneled a cup of coffee, threw on the equivalent of a bag lady's wardrobe, and ran around grabbing whatever didn't look like an expired lab experiment for lunch.

The only thing that I polished up to resemble a human quality was my teeth.

Good enough. Mad dash to get out the door.

Whoops.

Found my keys, almost forgot the children, still peaceful in their slumber.

No gentle, maternal wake-up call for them. Practically emptied the cereal box down their throats and poured what was left of the milk in for good measure and digestion. Manic and panic orders to brush their teeth and get Lanie's peacock-resembling hair into something that didn't look like a mad scientist undergoing electrocution.

Thank God Sean was there to offer to drive them to daycare. It gave me two seconds to breathe and discover that, although I work in a casual dress environment, forgetting to wear a bra would have been a tad too casual and might have caused people to talk.

I think yesterday, while dehydrating myself from crying from dawn to dusk, my brain matter leaked out of my cranium.

Have a great day y'all, and pay no attention to the blonde chick whose jeans are probably inside out and backwards. Just congratulate her on remembering to put her shoes on the right feet—even if she wore a slipper on the left and a pump on the right.

When I was a Kid, Grumble, Grumble

When I was a kid, adults used to bore me to tears with their long tales about how hard things were when they were growing up, what with walking twenty-five miles to school every morning ... uphill ... barefoot ... *both ways* ... yadda, yadda, yadda.

And I remember promising myself that when I grew up, there was no way in hell I was going to lay a bunch of crap like that on my kids about how hard I had it and how easy they've got it!

But now that I'm over the ripe old age of thirty, I can't help but look around and notice the youth of today. You've got it so easy! I mean, compared to my childhood, you live in a damn Utopia! And I hate to say it, but you kids today, you don't know how good you've got it!

I mean, when I was a kid, we didn't have the Internet. If we wanted to know something, we had to go to the damn library and look it up ourselves—in the card catalog!

There was no email! We had to actually write somebody a letter—with a pen! Then you had to walk all the way across the street and put it in the mailbox, and it would take like a week to get there! Stamps were 10 cents!

Child Protective Services didn't care if our parents beat us. As a matter of fact, the parents of all my friends also had permission to kick our ass! Nowhere was safe!

There were no MP3s or Napsters or iTunes! If you wanted to steal music, you had to hitchhike to the record store and shoplift it yourself!

Or you had to wait around all day to tape it off the radio, and the DJ would usually talk over the beginning and @#*% it all up! There were no CD players! We had tape decks in our car. We'd play our favorite tape and "eject" it when finished, and then the tape would come undone, rendering it useless. 'Cause, hey, that's how we rolled, Baby! Dig?

We didn't have fancy crap like call waiting! If you were on the phone and somebody else called, they got a busy signal, that's it!

There weren't any freakin' cell phones either. If you left the house, you just didn't make a damn call or receive one. You actually had to be out of touch with your "friends." *Oh my gosh!* Think of the horror … not being in touch with someone 24/7! And then there's *texting!* Yeah, right. Please! You kids have no idea how annoying you are.

And we didn't have fancy Caller ID either! When the phone rang, you had no idea who it was! It could be your school, your parents, your boss, your bookie, your drug dealer, the collection agent—you just didn't know! You had to pick it up and take your chances, mister!

We didn't have any fancy PlayStation or Xbox video games with high-resolution 3-D graphics! We had the Atari 2600! With games like "Space Invaders" and "Asteroids." Your screen guy was a little square! You actually had to use your imagination! And there were no multiple levels or screens. It was just one screen. Forever! And you could never win. The game just kept getting harder and harder and faster and faster until you died! Just like *life!*

You had to use a little book called a TV Guide to find out what was on TV! You were screwed when it came to channel surfing! You had to get off your ass and walk over to the TV to change the channel! *No Remotes!* Oh, no, what's the world coming to!?

There was no Cartoon Network either! You could only get cartoons on Saturday Morning. Do you hear what I'm saying? We had to wait *all week* for cartoons, you spoiled little rat-bastards!

And we didn't have microwaves. If we wanted to heat something up, we had to use the stove! Imagine that!

And our parents told us to stay outside and play … all day long! Oh, no—no electronics to soothe and comfort. And if you came back inside, you were doing chores!

And car seats … oh, please! Mom threw you in the back seat and you hung on. If you were lucky, you got the "safety arm" across the chest at the last moment if she had to stop suddenly, and if your head hit the dashboard, well that was your fault for calling "shot gun" in the first place!

See! That's exactly what I'm talking about! You kids today have it too easy. You're spoiled rotten! You guys wouldn't have lasted five minutes back in 1980s or any time before!

Even More Gratitude

With the Thanksgiving season approaching again, I wanted to count my blessings for ten straight days.

Day 1: Today I am thankful for my two healthy children when I am aware that there are families who can only pray for healthy children.

Day 2: Today I am thankful that I have my parents to show me all about what it means to persevere in love as they celebrate their wedding anniversary!

Day 3: Today I am thankful that my little boy left his television on all night even though I told him to shut it off before bed. It means I have power and warmth in my home, which I didn't have a year ago today.

Day 4: Today I need to be grateful to have a full-time job that keeps my children and me from going without when there are so many people out there who cannot find work to support their family. I need to remind myself of this more often. I also want to say that I am eternally grateful to have the knowledge that, despite all I have to give up, all the anguish with the ups and downs and all the times I have wanted to pull the covers over my head, my children are what completes me and the only two things in my life I have done right. Thanks to God for such amazing blessings!

Day 5: I am thankful for my sense of humor, as twisted as it may be at times. Laughter is truly the best medicine and has made the most horrific times in my life bearable. I will proudly enjoy a good dirty joke when I am ninety, God willing.

Day 6: Today I am grateful for the right to vote so that my voice will be heard.

Day 7: Right now, as I read such poisonous and profane posts written and displayed for all to read, by adults/parents who are the lead role models for their children, regarding their political views and attacking whomever had an opposing political vote with childish vulgarity ... (stopping to take a breath) ... I am thankful that I was raised by such classy parents who taught me the importance of being the bigger person and being someone who walks away from a negative situation with my head high and my integrity intact

Day 8: Today I am grateful like crazy for a school delay because I am *terrified* to drive my little Honda in this weather, and my drive to work is pretty long. At least with a delay, the roads have a better chance of being treated.

Day 9: As hard as my days at work can seem sometimes, I am so grateful that I have the good fortunate to work daily beside my teacher-partner in crime. She is an amazing inspiration and puts 110 percent into her work—even when her personal life is full of chaos and hardship. She helps make our most trying days worth fighting through by keeping me laughing and letting me act like me! Love her *substantially!*

Day 10: Today I am very thankful for the conversations I get to have with my Mom, both funny and serious. I don't have a lot of time to see my family face to face, so the talks on the phone are often therapeutic and humorous. I couldn't ask for more.

Good Things

After today's 504 education plan meeting, I had the need to talk with my little man.

To talk about the fact that his grades were above the charts (4 A+'s and 3 A's) and that he didn't need all A+'s to be amazing.

To talk about how he deals with stress within school. How he's come so far and proved the professional "theories" so wrong about the so-called "rules" that accompany individuals on the spectrum:

He is outgoing.

He has intense empathy for others.

He has a sense of humor unlike most.

He owns his differences in ways I am envious of.

My son rocks his autism.

My son owns who he is and what he has to offer to his world.

And do you know how he ended our conversation?

"Everyone in the world is exceptional. I mean, everyone is smart in their own things. Some people at school are rude, but that's because they don't know yet that they are probably not doing the things that they are good at. They don't know that they are exceptional at things like other people. Some people, like me, are so lucky to be weird."

This is where I choked up and became belligerent.

"Don't you *ever* call yourself weird again! You are the most inspiring person I know."

Logan: "No, Mom. People who are weird are the ones who do things different. Not like the other kids. Weird is a good thing. Weird people are the kind of people who see good stuff and want to be nicer people. I like thinking I'm a weird kid. It makes me look at kids who aren't nice and think that they haven't found out yet that they have good things to learn about themselves. You always say that there are bullies. I know that. But I think they just need to have other kids show them how to be kind. That's what makes me not care that I'm weird."

And just like that, I thanked God even more for giving me a child who teaches me about humankind.

Fashion Statement

Thought I'd share a moment in the life of me that simply could've been horrifying.

So yesterday, I was at the reception of a beautiful wedding. I was feeling pretty good about myself: dress, heels, makeup done right.

I was leaving the ladies room and decided to take one last glance in the mirror, thinking, "Yup, Trisha, you've still got it." And to just let everyone know, I'm not a vain person in the least. It was just one of those moments in a woman's life that gives reassurance. The "girls" were looking fine and my hair was under some control rather than being tamed by the everyday ponytail.

To put it blatantly, I was feeling hot as hell. I got ready to make my entrance back into the crowd of wedding patrons.

And thank you God for making me glance due south.

For this sexy chick was dragging a good two feet of toilet paper from the heel of my shoes.

It could've gone *sooo* wrong. So very wrong.

Somehow the sexy desirable level I was feeling radiating from my head to my toes dissipated a little.

Just a little.

I am humble enough to admit my near epic fail at being the confident MILF chick I was so trying to convey.

The Original Cool Mom

I'm looking at a photo of my mother and me from 1997 … I was 20 years old, and it was the first time I saw that my mom was pretty damn cool. I may or have may not have had my fair share of alcoholic beverages at my cousin's wedding with her raising an eyebrow in disapproval—but acceptance. We settled our disagreement over a few stogies while the sun set over the balcony at the reception.

Flash forward to the present time. There have been far more than eyebrows raised at my choices. For the sake of keeping my mother's hives and anxiety at bay, I won't delve into my tattoos, piercings, adrenaline-inducing antics (the ones that I was able to cross off my bucket list), and everything else that has made her thankful for Xanax. In many ways, I am so different from my mother in these colorful aspects that make me unique.

Yet, I am so grateful to say that my mother has given me so many of her own incredible traits. I have her sense of sick humor, her ability to find so much empathy in the struggles of others, the gift of perseverance and determination in getting even the most challenging things I covet in the world, and the world's best training in motherhood.

So much of my life I owe to my mom. In the hardest times, not only did she never give up on me, but she also forced me to find strength within myself to push forward. In the best of times, she celebrated with me and has never ceased to laugh at my sick and twisted (and frankly, hilarious) views in the world.

I feel for those who don't have a mom for a best friend like mine. Happy Mother's Day, Jeanie Hall! Because I love you, one particular Panera Bread story will remain locked away in my head, so that when I am blue, I can simply picture the facial expression on the person who you were in contact with during that event, and find some kind of empathy for the lopsided situation that you certainly must have dealt with all day (insert Winky face icon here!).

And Yet …

You know what? Screw this negative funk I'm in.

I need to get away from the computer where I have spent endless hours these past few days sending out résumé after résumé, creating the perfect LinkedIn account, job searching and researching, and making endless phone calls.

So what if the furnace needed to be fixed today? If anyone knows me, I fight first and cry later. Proactive woman called the right people who came out and fixed it. Problem solved. Next?

I guess I can't complain because the mere fact that I had a furnace issue comes down to finding inner-gratitude that I have a home to have a furnace issue.

Yes, life has been on its own crappy terms with me this past week. I'm not gonna lie. I've cried more, slept less. and found myself in more distress and panic these past few days than I can ever remember experiencing.

And yet … call it a character flaw or call it driven passion for success, I know I will get through this. After all, Supermoms don't take life's low blows lying down. I won't give up until all the pieces are put back together.

And on that note …

I've decided to tear my behind from my laptop and put today's energies into the reasons for why I am working so hard to better the situation: my children. What could *ever* be more important to a weary and struggling mother than her miraculous creations.

So, movie tickets to 4:35 showing of *The Lego Movie* are already purchased, and I will be there to scoop them up when they step off that school bus to surprise them with the news.
I really should do this more often. Damn, it feels amazing to look forward to the innocent happiness that only my children can move in me.

Lions and Tigers and Biomes, Oh My

After hours of hysterical crying from my son and my constant reassurance that him missing one day of school won't cause him to "fail and give up," it's safe to say that we both would ace a science exam on biomes, abiotic examples, and ways in which biomes have comparable biotics.

I hate to be nasty, but how in the effing hell did we come to a place within the educational requirements of sixth-grade students where the homework is such that, after nearly two hours, a child is this stressed about the material? I understand the curriculum requirements and standards that are supposed to be implemented within our children's academic lives, but I am really uneasy with the fact that I have a child who is stressed to no return because of the workload he has to bring home.

If he were in high school, I could possibly rest easier. But, sixth grade is far too early for children to cry themselves to hysteria because they feel so overwhelmed.

I'm so tired that I'm afraid I'm going to brush my teeth with hair gel. However, I now know my shit in the biome and abiotic/biotic world of sixth-grade ecology.

On a silver lining note, at least I only have hair products to make the blunder with brushing and not hemorrhoid cream.

If I go to bed with Axe breath, I suppose it's better than *ass* breath.

Kitty, Kitty, Kitty

Sometimes I'm jealous of my own life.

For instance, I bet most of you didn't spend a half hour before the sun came up this Wednesday morning crawling around playing everybody's favorite pre-work game, "Find Where the New Kitten Crapped in Your Bedroom."

I mean, not *everyone* is lucky enough to have such tender, glamorous moments to brag about.

P.S.: After nearly fainting from excessive sniffing on all fours trying to locate the foul present from the kitten, I won the bonus round when I successfully found the (dry-heaving insertion) cat dump to end all cat dumps neatly hidden in my *clean laundry*.

"What do we have for our contestant?"

Oh let's run a load of laundry with enough detergent to clean a water buffalo followed by a floor scrubbing with questionable mixtures of household cleansers so as not to invite kitty back to what she perceived as a super comfy latrine.

I may or may not have spewed a slew of profanities at the cat before sending her downstairs for the rest of the day. Everyone knows that felines understand the F-bomb.

Gee, I can't wait to enjoy my breakfast.

Neetzy

A million memories can be made in fifteen years. A first home, a marriage, two miracle babies born, struggles, tears, a friendship stronger after a divorce, millions of laughs, memories from life's beginnings and finales.

When our fifteen-year-old kitty Anita passed away this morning, she took with her the gift of those memories. To some, losing a beloved pet is part of life. However, for me, losing my little friend feels like losing a big part of my past.

You see, fifteen years ago, before any of those memories were even the glimmer of an idea, I was living with my parents, unsure of who or where my future self would be. I did know however, that along with her sweet and furry brother, Anita would become part of my life. I was completely unaware that my sweet, fresh little fur baby would follow me on such a long and fulfilling journey.

She was loved. I know in my heart, aside from the raw pain I am feeling now, that she left this world knowing that she just "fit" perfectly into our lives.

Anita, my "Neetzy," I pray that rainbow bridge leads you to everything you loved with us.

And that you finally catch the dot on the wall.

Random Randomness, Part Nine, 2018

I hate emotions.

I swear like a sailor and can always put anyone's filthy humor to shame.

I believe I was born with a men's mentality and a touch of that girly shit that makes me a strong soldier with the ability to put my face on in the morning and feign a strong woman.

Damn. Sometimes, though.

Sometimes I wonder if there will be a participation trophy for me at the end. Lord knows I have given it my all.

This grown-up thing bestowed upon me had truly put one hell of a damper on who I once envisioned my adult existence to be.

Tomorrow will be a new day.

***

And on snow day nights, they love each other just long enough to rob one another's banks and giggle.

And I become all right with the world for the moment.

I love these two with all that I have. These are the awful years that books never prepared me for.

But once in a miracle moment, they prove how much they could never live without the other.

My silver lining for today came within me peeking on a brother versus sister Monopoly game—with laughter and the love that comes with a tentative teen/preteen sibling truce in life.

No school tomorrow. Let them be little for a little while longer.

Mom loves you most.

As the song says, "In my life, I have loved you more."

***

Have you ever thought about the fact that there are some sentences that have probably never been uttered throughout the ages?

For instance, "It would be so satisfying to shave a chicken" has probably never been declared verbally by anybody. And why would it? Who would actually have such a thought move from their cranium and exit their mouths?

Well, ponder no longer. My morning drive to my children's bus stop was made so much more entertaining.

Because, well, Dylanie.

Disclaimer: Use caution when leaving my daughter around live poultry.

***

If I won the lottery, I would take care of my parents, brother, and children's future and the lives of everyone else I love.

Then … I'd buy Maine beachfront property in Old Orchard Beach for the summer and South Carolina beachfront property for the winter. I'd make it all accessible for my dad so my family could enjoy it with me.

And ass implants.

Definitely ass implants.

The rest I would be frivolous with!

***

I'm in a mood after an emotional week.

I'm in a mood.

I'm in a mood that has caused me to order a pizza just for me, light some candles, and chill out in a jacuzzi while listening to some inspirational music.

It's been a long and emotional week for so many people. We all need pizza and a massaging bath.

***

I'm so glad this week is over.

This was one for the books of suckiest, sad, and anxiety-written chapters I've had in a while.

I've learned that I am so thankful for my family this week.

And I've learned how I have the partial ability to function as an adult on obscenely small amounts of sleep.

***

I just sat my daughter down and had this conversation:

The spoken word can cut like a knife and leave one in self-doubt eternally.

The spoken word, in the most beautiful form can make others believe in themselves and start the ball rolling to make a change.

I believe in teaching how much one small utterance or action done with kindness might be the only aspect in people's lives that makes them believe in themselves.

We can be the change, one soul at a time.

***

You know you are in desperate need of sleep when you stop at the gas station and, while discussing the upcoming snowstorm with the older gentleman who rang you up, you mistakenly tell him how much you were looking forward to the warmer days when you can drive around with your top off.

I'm not sure if I just made his day or gave him a reason to find a therapist.

***

Me to my daughter: "Have you heard about any new stupid challenges like the Tide Pod type of challenge? Something about putting something in your nose?"

Dylanie: "What challenge now? Wait! Like the condom challenge?"

Me: "Uh, yes. that's the one. Have you heard about it at school?"

Eye roll from the pre-teen.

Dylanie: "The condom challenge was *so* 2016, Mom! Besides, the only thing I've ever seen someone stick up their nose that wasn't okay was a Barbie stiletto."

Well, I guess this conversation was a success.

Right?

Please tell me I'm doing okay as a mom … and then feed me.

***

Just passed an older gentleman by the Enfield library on the side the road taking a whiz in the bushes without a care in the world as to who saw him.

I don't know if I am horrified or jealous of the few cares that he actually gives.

***

I cannot stop craving V-8.

It's driving me insane because the gas station next to me doesn't carry it.

I could drink a gallon right now.

Somebody has to love me enough to tell me where I can get my hands on some in the morning.

If not, this could be my last post as I will surely be deprived of whatever is in such a magical vegetable concoction.

***

Does it make anyone else absolutely irate when you take a sharp turn while driving and your purse or bag tips and spills all of your crap into the dark vortex of hell under the seats? Or into the space between the center console that no human hand can fit into for retrieval?

I think I just spewed every foul word in the human language in no particular order or reason.

At least the V-8 was unscathed.

***

It's such an isolating feeling when you feel like the only person in the world who overthinks to a degree where it feels like you are driving 100 m.p.h. with enough fuel to sustain you a mere drive around the block.

***

You know your daughter has your genes when you can watch the end of *Titanic* and not mention each other's attempts to squelch the throat lumps and hasty tears being wiped away.

***

Just threatened my kids with me singing Disney classics all night if the dishes aren't done.

They are strong willed but I am stronger.

***

When your own mom tells you what a good mother you are … *ahhhh*.

Sometimes, I need to know that someone else sees me and that I am not messing up, that I am trying so damn hard with all that I have. I love my mom. She just knows.

***

You know you are in desperate straits and that you've taken the path less followed in the mom maze of life when you have to reprimand your eleven-year-old daughter because you heard this:

"To the window, to the window, to the wall, to the …"

"Dylanie Sue, don't let me hear that again! Do you read me?"

And what does she do?

She laughs and tells me that I don't even know what she was singing.

Pretty sure there's only one version, and I'm about to send this child to a damn convent.

When I was eleven, I was riding a bike with the neighborhood boys and still excited by the ice cream truck.

There wasn't a thought about the windows or the walls.

And I don't think I even knew or wanted to know the rest.

***

Ya know, I'm feeling Happy Meals are in order as pre-movie early dinners. Haters need not comment. I am fully aware of the vortex of negative factual aspects that arise when one mentions the Golden Arches on a social media site. However, Betty Crocker, Donna Reed, Mother Teresa, I am not. I am human and

I am a kick-ass mother. Plus, I steal their fries when they lose focus and spot something shiny. Or a bird. Squirrel!

***

Advice if I may …

Under *no* circumstances should you ever bring your children to Five Below to "look" for beach items to buy at a later date.

I was in an "F-it" mood and didn't want to deal with the whining. No beach items were purchased on this endeavor.

On another note, my daughter got over me threatening to punish her for acting a fool and couldn't wait to inflate her new chair.

Inside the damn car.

***

No matter how many PPT meetings I have attended in my children's life, I always get so nervous before they begin. I guess the anxiety comes from not knowing if I'm going to turn into a fierce beast or if I'm going to get my point across.

In other words, if I'm going to get my own way without throwing a major fit.

I never know if these meetings are going to be quick and painless or if I am going to have to sign up for AARP by the time they are over.

***

Daughter: "So there's these boys who all say they really like me. Maybe I should ask to move my seat in those classes. One says he loves me."

Mom: …

…

…

Nope.

* Cues *Scarface* quotes. *
Just. *No.*

***

Parent hack #103: When you are out of margarita mix for your tequila, ginger ale and tears work fine.

***

Dylanie: "Oh my God, Mommy! Dunkin Donuts has the 'F' word on their donut bag!"
Me: "I'm sure it's not the "F-word," Lanie."
Dylanie: "I'm not kidding Mommy. They really put it on there. Read it. It's right here. (Points to alleged profanity inscribed on bag.)
Me (giggling): "Lanie, that says 'zero trans fat.'"
Dylanie: "Yeah that's the "F-word" and you just said it out loud. (Turns to the other room where her brother is playing.)
Dylanie: "Logan, Mommy's sayin' the 'F-word' out loud!"
Shaking my head, yet again …

***

Nothing says family breakfast time like the Muller siblings having a contest to see who can come up with the most terms pertaining to the word vomit.
Pass the cereal, please.

***

I told myself that I was going on vacation and I wasn't going to think about anything that is a responsibility back home. I was just going to relax and enjoy myself.
Also me … Walked two miles today to find the perfect rocks and shells to bring back for my students. I'm so excited to share

with them the treasures that I've collected and to do fun projects with them the next time I back at the, you know, job responsibilities.

***

Parents ... a question: How much energy would *you* put into worrying about the worst-case scenario if your eight-year-old daughter informed you about her immense desire to sample the cat treats because they "smell wonderful."

Umm ... yeah ... anyone?

That's kinda normal, right? No?

Anyone?

... and speaking of the cat ...

Dylanie just informed me that her underwear fits the family cat perfectly.

Guess keeping a closer eye on the kitty is the new item on my to-do list.

***

Took a walk on the beach with my son a little while ago. It amazes me that he is as tall as me when I think of him as a two-year-old running down the beach in a pull-up diaper.

Then he says to me something that leveled me in such a weird, random, and humorous way.

A plane went by with one of those signs trailing it advertising a local establishment.

Logan: "Want to hear something weird?"

Me: "Always."

Logan: "Sometimes when I see those planes fly by, I picture it carrying a sign from a pissed-off husband with the words, "Screw you, Janis."

I don't know why he chose Janis, but I'd hate to make her man angry.

Did I mention how much I adore that young man?

***

So I was telling Logan he needs to find a broom and sweep the floor, and he can't tell the difference between a broom and a Swiffer.

And so I tell him, "You know, Logan, you're going to have a home someday. You're going to be a grown-up."

And he replied, smiling at his already grown-up sense of irony, "But am I though? But am I?"

And I said, "Get to work."

How can I domesticate this child?

***

Random young girl in the Mexican restaurant as I picked up our supper: "Oh my God I love your hair. How do you get it like that?"

Me: "I pray to God every day and curse the devil for a miracle to make me not look like Diana Ross."

Random girl (has no words regarding my insane mane): "Your total is $31.87."

Don't comment on the do unless you want the sad truth.

***

At least I was the mother hen amongst my friends when I was devious as a teenager.

Skeeve Alert!

Anyone who knows me knows I have major OCD with a lot of things that other people might shrug off as minuscule and unimportant. I'm a germophobe, a relentless worrier about my "to do lists," and petrified of anything resembling a living worm.

You get the picture.

I also have a major thing about teeth. Brushing, flossing, regular dental maintenance—anything related to healthy choppers. So you can understand why I get so skeeved out when little ones in my classroom pull out their loose, dangling, bloody baby teeth in my vicinity. Even writing about it makes me cringe and shudder.

Yet I learned the other day that when a child comes up to you with sheer glee and announces that they finally had success in ripping off their wart—well, I can honestly say I would take a bloody incisor any day over the knowledge that there was a wart on the loose in the classroom, its whereabouts unknown.

My response? Well, what else could I say to that?

"Please go wash your hands thoroughly and use the hand sanitizer when you're done."

I mean, *really?* Now I have to think about all the skin abnormalities that are discarded on the floor by sweet little children.

I'm wondering if a hazmat suit is appropriate attire in the school system.

Do-Over

Lately, I have found my attitude about life kinda miserable and unsatisfactory. Many times a day, I've been pondering the causes of these feelings and their effects on my life. It's led me to question whether or not, if given the opportunity, I would want a do-over. I think the answer came to me this morning.

It depends on the situation.

If I had the chance to change the detrimental situations that were beyond my control (family illness, any diagnoses, etc), I wouldn't go back and change the course of events. As tough as those issues have been, they have made me so much stronger and more aware of the love I have for my family and what is truly important.

As for the situations I have control over that are making me want to stay in bed, I have the blessing of having a chance to make the most of my life. I have way too much going for me (education, personal knowledge, and strong work and life ethics) to continue on this dead-end path.

We make our own do-overs. Do-over begins now.

Perspective

With another school year approaching, my maternal emotional turmoil returns tenfold. As my children get older, the wrenching realization that I can't protect them from the evils in the world as I could when they were babies tortures me. I can only pray that I have instilled into their little minds what amazing people they are and that nothing is impossible if they refuse to give up.

I accept that my son may never be an athletic icon, as he is simply Logan: a sweet, bright little boy with an imagination and intelligence that will take him places. I can't force where those places will be. My daughter may never be a mathematician, but her amazing wit and love for animals and nature proves that she is full of surprises and immeasurable compassion.

I won't lie and say there aren't times when I envy the parents of the little league champ or the elementary academic scholar of the year. But then I see the news teeming with stories of missing children and devastated tears on parents whose child is terminally ill or will never spend another Christmas morning watching the magic on those tiny faces when they realize Santa really came.

I don't need the trophies and honor roll bumper stickers to realize that my children are amazing and perfect with all their imperfections.

Aren't we all?

Blessings

I need to share this.

I don't have all that I had wanted in life when I was planning my grown-up years. However, who else can say that they are so truly blessed with parents and a brother who would stop on a dime and come to my aid when I need it, children who sometimes I find myself staring in adoration at the amazing, kind, funny and thoughtful little people they are becoming, friends who bring me back from the brink with love and tons of humor, a great friendship and teammate with my ex-husband who is an amazing dad to our children and for Sean, a man who works his fingers to the bone day in an day out to make sure this family is never without—and never forgets to tell and show us how important we are in his life.

It's the things in life that aren't things but rather blessings that I sometimes need to sit back and say, "Trisha, life on life's terms, and your life is full of everything you need."

It's not easy to say how much I love the people in my life, as I am not wired to feel comfortable in verbalizing it. But, in my own way, as my ex would call it, my "flighty shit I post on Facebook," I just needed to share my wealth.

Dear Seventeen-Year-Old Trisha

I am sitting here staring at your face. A face with a smile so obviously forced … peering up at me through that shiny page of your senior yearbook.

Page twenty to be precise.

A page within a book that was dedicated to having your adolescent existence permanently stamped as proof that you survived what you thought were going to be the hardest years. A page and a picture that was once so important. A face with a forced smile that never knew the life that would become a reality after the pages of that book were signed by friends you would most likely never speak to again.

Now, forgive me if that initial comment sounded harsh. Forgive me for the lecture that is about to ensue. Squelch the eye rolling for a moment and understand that what I am about to tell you is the cold hard truth. If I could be there to hold your hand, I would sit you down and bring you a coffee. You need to be open minded, aware, and willing within your soul to accept what I am about to bestow upon you.

I am you. I am you—looking down the barrel of forty years old. I am who you will become in almost twenty-three years from the day that picture was taken. I won't get into the physical attributes that have changed since that picture when you were seventeen. Not yet at least. The outer aspects of seventeen-year-old you are just the rough draft of a canvas that will weather over time. They are but merely the early edition of a book which will someday become a hardcover. Not necessarily the bestseller you dreamed it would become, but harder than you ever imagined you could be at seventeen.

I am you twenty-three years later. You are going to be okay.

That picture on page twenty.

That girl on page twenty with the eyebrows that had never seen a wax or tweezers. That girl whose picture was probably airbrushed because of blemishes that were far overblown in the realms of a seventeen-year-old girl's priorities.

We need to talk.

Let's start with that first broken heart. You weren't going to listen to anyone who tried talking to you about the fact that being in love in your teen years would probably not end up in the fairy tale way that you had dreamed it would play out. You shunned friends and family who insisted that you had your whole life to settle down with one individual. In your mind, there wasn't a life beyond the two of you.

Who could blame you? Three years with your first love is an eternity at seventeen. Hell, it's longer than most Hollywood marriages nowadays. It was more than photo sessions and private jokes. More than love notes folded into triangles and passed in the hallways. More than a facet of mere puppy love that it was often whittled down to in the eyes of others.

And yet, not long before the picture on page twenty was captured through the lens of the camera, it ended. I remember it well, as I should. It was right after Thanksgiving around the time the holiday cheer should have come upon you. I won't dig up bad memories as to how it went down, for I don't need to. At seventeen, it is still fresh and raw within your psyche.

When he left you that evening, he took with him everything you had believed to be what your life was supposed to entail. Everything beautiful, trustworthy, sane, warm, peaceful and safe. An open wound exposed to a jarring, salty overflow of morbid reality.

The emptiest void, you thought.

I can still see you during those first few days. Refusing to leave your bed and needing your mother more than you ever had needed her in the past. How your heart would jump into your throat every time the phone would ring, imagining him on the line proclaiming that he had made the mistake of an eternity. The way your heart would drop in a place you didn't know existed within you when his voice never greeted you upon answering. Feeling like you would never find it in yourself to eat or sleep again.

I can still see you during those first few days. Refusing to leave your bed and needing your mother more than you ever had needed her in the past. How your heart would jump into your throat every time the phone would ring, imagining him on the other line proclaiming that he had made the mistake of an eternity. The way your heart would drop in a place you didn't know existed within you when his voice never greeted you upon answering. Feeling like you would never find it in yourself to eat or sleep again.

That call didn't come. At least not when you thought you needed it to.

You learned to fake a smile, fake an appetite … fake the normalcies within your daily existence with the faith that you'd get through a pain that left scars in places that only the soul could see.

I wish I could go back and make you understand why the absence of that phone call was God's plan. Yes, it broke your soul and made you turn your back on His faith and love. At 17, you were far too jaded, too young, too stubborn … too ignorant to believe that your life was just beginning.

That the phone call that never came was a gift.

A gift that would eventually give you strength to move forward and begin the next, amazing, trying, beautiful, horrible, insightful and humbling chapters that made up the story of Trisha.

I wish I could show you, at 17, how amazing you are during these chapters … twenty plus years later.

I wish I could promise that girl on page 20 that she would persevere and find strength, acceptance and love for herself.

That life is going to happen on its terms and there will be times when it will feel dark and hopeless. Those times will be life changing and filled with fear and anguish. They will be frequent and will challenge your faith in finding any silver linings within your story.

You'll grow from pain. You'll find those silver linings. This I promise.

And Trisha, you just wait (and hold on tight for the ride). All I can say is that today's chapter contains a tired mother at her wits end with two beautiful children. She's 13 and he's 15. There are hormones, pimples, braces, late night trips to buy the "right tampons," band practice, drama practice, scouts, soccer and attitudes. These, today, are somehow all your fault and responsibility. Just ride it out.

It's an amazing ride that you will come to love and never imagine anything else before you buckled up for the journey.

Your life didn't end that year on page 20. You were just beginning a rough draft that would someday be your own best seller. I promise this on your own children. You'll see.

Love,
Trisha

P.S. The call that never came … he's bald now. You're welcome.

Acknowledgements

First and foremost, I need to thank God for somehow making me comfortable in believing that the world needed my very colorful existence. For bestowing within me the abilities to view my personal universe "outside the box."* (Lord, that box must contain the missing filters for every eccentric, awkward, inappropriate and profane moment that gave me great material to be put into the written word).

*Warning—don't open the box if you are faint of heart. Trust me on this one.

An enormous amount of gratitude needs to be given to my friend and former college professor, John Sheirer. This book would probably never have come to fruition without his constant drive and perseverance to force me to believe in my abilities to share my crazy world through my writing. Whenever I doubted myself, he was there to kick my behind and remind me of my passion for writing and how much the world needed to see a more raw, albeit real life, humorous side to what became of our lives when we thought we had everything all planned out. Humor that is so needed within a world that has become so hell bent on the negative aspects surrounding us. Humor that finally made it to the printed page even when I was terrified to take the leap, "bird by bird."

A special thank you to Jessica Handly who saw that I had something special. Something in the concrete written word that would help others relate and find realistic humor within real life experiences that come with … well, real life. Without her, this book would still be a pipe dream.

And to my family—especially my parents. I could never have made this possible without living, with you, through "all the feelings". If not for you always having my back and being my biggest fans … I'd still be just a woman whose posts always prompted Mom to beg me to not post the material that was too damn crazy funny to keep to myself. Like I've learned throughout the years, if you can't laugh at the hard times … all that is left to do is cry. Thank you for always being my sounding board and understanding the benefits of laughter. Thank you for believing in me. "In this life, I love you more."

And what would this book be without my children and all that they bring to the table within my world? My children saved my life in ways that even I couldn't put into words. On the toughest days, my children shine through as the miracles they became from the first day they were placed in my arms. As rocky as our world has been throughout this journey together, we fill the tough cracks with so much love and laughter. You will never know how much I thank God every day that he chose me to be your Mom.

About the Author

Trisha Hall-Muller is a lifelong resident of Connecticut where she lives with her two children (the miracle minions that helped bless this book with the 💩 she couldn't make up if she tried). She attended Asnuntuck Community College and Central Connecticut State University where she received her B.S. in Elementary Education with a concentration in English. In her spare time, she enjoys Facebooking, vacationing in Old Orchard Beach, Maine, spending time with her family, and advocating for Autism Awareness. This is her first (and hopefully not last) book.

Made in the USA
Middletown, DE
11 April 2024

52864127R00115